AIR FRYER RECIPES
FOR BEGINNERS

Over than 250 Complete Recipes to Prepare Quick and Appetizing Dishes for Healthy Eating

SAM HAMIL

Table of Contents

Sommario

Introduction

What is an air fryer?

It is an appliance that typically has an egg shape, more or less square, with a removable basket in which you put the food to be cooked. It takes advantage of the concept of air cooking at high temperatures that reach up to 200° allowing a healthy "frying-not-frying" of fresh food. Abandon, then, the thought of frying in which the food is immersed in a lot of oil because the amount of oil used inside the air fryer can be as little as a couple of teaspoons of spray. True frying in lots of hot oil is practically "dangerous", especially in case you abuse it or don't pay proper attention. In the air fryer, the oil will never reach the smoke point and is therefore not harmful.

The hot air, which reaches high temperatures, circulates in the compartment of the air fryer allowing even cooking of food both outside and inside. This way you can cook meat, fish, vegetables and thousands of other dishes in no time - in short, you can prepare many recipes with the air fryer. Meat cooked in the air fryer is succulent, tender, and soft, excess fat runs off and does not remain inside the meat giving it an exceptional flavor.

The air fryer also works as an oven and grill...

The air fryer is very different and in addition to its main purpose, the air cooking of food for a light and healthy fried, it is also an appliance that serves as an oven for gratin for different recipes, pasta dishes, vegetables, to prepare cakes and pies of all kinds, muffins, buns, pizzas. It has been shown that in the best performing models, the air fryer allows eliminating excess fat, even up to 50%, without altering the flavor of food, giving the right friability typical of fried foods.

Which air fryer to choose to buy?

For air fryer selection, the suggestion could also be a reliable product to urge better and better results. A high-quality product makes an equivalent quality product. Therefore, it would be fair to consider spending a bit more on a much better-performing air fryer that also has better quality materials. However, depending on your needs, many excellent products are affordable.

Now you just need to take a look at the air fryer recipes. They are all proven, safe and outstanding recipes!

Chicken

Asian Chicken Legs

(Ready in about 15 minutes + marinating time | Servings 3)

333 Calories; 17.6g Fat; 10.4g Carbs; 32.8g Protein; 8.1g Sugars

Ingredients

1/4 cup soy sauce
1 teaspoon brown mustard
1 teaspoon garlic paste
2 tablespoons tomato paste
2 tablespoons sesame oil
1 tablespoon brown sugar
2 tablespoons rice vinegar
1 pound chicken drumettes

Directions

Place the chicken drumettes and the other ingredients in a resalable bag; allow it to marinate for 2 hours.

Discard the marinade and transfer the chicken drumettes to the Air Fryer cooking basket.

Cook at 400 degrees F for 12 minutes, shaking the basket halfway through the cooking time to ensure even cooking.

In the meantime, bring the reserved marinade to a boil in a small saucepan. Immediately turn the heat to low and let it simmer until the sauce has reduced by half.

Spoon the sauce over the chicken drumettes and serve immediately.

Classic Chicken Legs

(Ready in about 30 minutes | Servings 3)

347 Calories; 9.1g Fat; 11.3g Carbs; 41g Protein; 0.1g Sugars

Ingredients

1/3 cup all-purpose flour
1/2 teaspoon ground white pepper
1 teaspoon seasoning salt
1 teaspoon garlic paste
1 teaspoon rosemary
1 whole egg + 1 egg white
6 chicken drumettes
1 heaping tablespoon fresh chives, chopped

Directions

Start by preheating your Air Fryer to 390 degrees.
Mix the flour with white pepper, salt, garlic paste, and rosemary in a small-sized bowl.
In another bowl, beat the eggs until frothy.
Dip the chicken into the flour mixture, then into the beaten eggs; coat with the flour mixture one more time.
Cook the chicken drumettes for 22 minutes. Serve warm, garnished with chives.

Roasted Sausage and Carrots

(Ready in about 20 minutes | Servings 3)

313 Calories; 13.6g Fat; 14.7g Carbs; 32.3g Protein; 7.2g Sugars

Ingredients

1 pound chicken sausages, smoked
1 pound carrots, trimmed and halved lengthwise
1 tablespoon Dijon mustard
2 tablespoons olive oil
1/2 teaspoon sea salt
1/4 teaspoon ground black pepper

Directions

Start by preheating your Air Fryer to 380 degrees F. Pierce the sausages all over with a fork and add them to the cooking basket. Add the carrots and the remaining ingredients; toss until well coated. Cook for 10 minutes in the preheated Air Fryer. Shake the basket and cook an additional 5 to 7 minutes. Serve warm.

Tebasaki

(Ready in about 25 minutes + marinating time | Servings 2)

344 Calories; 18.8g Fat; 8.4g Carbs; 28.4g Protein; 3.7g Sugars

Ingredients

4 chicken drumettes
1 tablespoon sesame oil
1 tablespoon black vinegar
2 tablespoons soy sauce
1 tablespoon ginger juice
2 tablespoons sake
1 tablespoon sesame seeds, lightly toasted

Directions

Place all ingredients, except for the sesame oil, in a glass bowl. Cover, transfer to your refrigerator and let it marinate for 1 hour.
Cook in the preheated Air Fryer at 370 degrees F for 22 minutes until golden brown; baste and turn them over halfway through the cooking time.
Serve garnished with toasted sesame seeds.

Sausage and Ham

(Ready in about 45 minutes | Servings 4)

509 Calories; 20.1g Fat; 40g Carbs; 41.2g Protein; 3.9g Sugars

Ingredients

1/2 pound chicken sausages, smoked
1/2 pound ham, sliced
6 ounces hash browns, frozen and shredded
2 garlic cloves, minced
8 ounces spinach
1/2 cup Ricotta cheese
1/2 cup Asiago cheese, grated
4 eggs
1/2 cup yogurt
1/2 cup milk
Salt and ground black pepper, to taste
1 teaspoon smoked paprika

Directions

Start by preheating your Air Fryer to 380 degrees F. Cook the sausages and ham for 10 minutes; set aside.

Meanwhile, in a preheated saucepan, cook the hash browns and garlic for 4 minutes, stirring frequently; remove from the heat, add the spinach and cover with the lid.

Allow the spinach to wilt completely. Transfer the sautéed mixture to a baking pan. Add the reserved sausage and ham.

In a mixing dish, thoroughly combine the cheese, eggs, yogurt, milk, salt, pepper, and paprika. Pour the cheese mixture over the hash browns in the pan.

Place the baking pan in the cooking basket and cook approximately 30 minutes or until everything is thoroughly cooked. Bon appétit!

Chicken Drumsticks with Blue Cheese Sauce

(Ready in about 25 minutes | Servings 4)

246 Calories; 20g Fat; 1.5g Carbs; 14.2g Protein; 0.2g Sugars

Ingredients

1/2 teaspoon shallot powder
1/2 teaspoon garlic powder
1/2 teaspoon coriander
1/4 teaspoon red pepper flakes
Sea salt and ground black pepper, to season
2 chicken drumsticks, skinless and boneless
1/4 cup blue cheese, softened
4 tablespoons mayonnaise
4 tablespoons sour cream
1 teaspoon fresh garlic, pressed
1 teaspoon fresh lime juice

Directions

In a resealable bag, place the shallot powder, garlic powder, coriander, red pepper, salt and black pepper; add in the chicken drumsticks and shake until they are well coated.
Spritz the chicken drumsticks with a nonstick cooking oil and place in the cooking basket.
Air fry the chicken drumsticks at 370 degrees F for 20 minutes, turning them over halfway through the cooking time.
Meanwhile, make the sauce by whisking the remaining ingredients. Place the sauce in your refrigerator until ready to serve.
Serve the chicken drumsticks with blue cheese sauce. Bon appétit!

Meatballs with Cheese

(Ready in about 15 minutes | Servings 4)

497 Calories; 24g Fat; 20.7g Carbs; 41.9g Protein; 4.1g Sugars

Ingredients

1 pound ground turkey
1/2 pound ground pork
1 egg, well beaten
1 cup seasoned breadcrumbs
1 teaspoon dried basil
1 teaspoon dried rosemary
1/4 cup Manchego cheese, grated
2 tablespoons yellow onions, finely chopped
1 teaspoon fresh garlic, finely chopped
Sea salt and ground black pepper, to taste

Directions

In a mixing bowl, combine all the ingredients until everything is well incorporated.

Shape the mixture into 1-inch balls.

Cook the meatballs in the preheated Air Fryer at 380 degrees for 7 minutes. Shake halfway through the cooking time. Work in batches. Serve with your favorite pasta. Bon appétit!

Turkey Wings with Roasted Potatoes

(Ready in about 55 minutes | Servings 4)

567 Calories; 14.3g Fat; 65.7g Carbs; 46.1g Protein; 2.9g Sugars

Ingredients

4 large-sized potatoes, peeled and cut into 1-inch chunks
1 tablespoon butter, melted
1 teaspoon rosemary
1 teaspoon garlic salt
1/2 teaspoon ground black pepper
1 ½ pounds turkey wings
2 tablespoons olive oil
2 garlic cloves, minced
1 tablespoon Dijon mustard
1/2 teaspoon cayenne pepper

Directions

Add the potatoes, butter, rosemary, salt, and pepper to the cooking basket.
Cook at 400 degrees F for 12 minutes. Reserve the potatoes, keeping them warm.
Now, place the turkey wings in the cooking basket that is previously cleaned and greased with olive oil. Add the garlic, mustard, and cayenne pepper.
Cook in the preheated Air Fryer at 350 degrees f for 25 minutes. Turn them over and cook an additional 15 minutes.
Test for doneness with a meat thermometer. Serve with warm potatoes.

Chicken and Cheese Stuffed Mushrooms

(Ready in about 15 minutes | Servings 4)

166 Calories; 8.2g Fat; 3.4g Carbs; 19.1g Protein; 2.3g Sugars

Ingredients

9 medium-sized button mushrooms, cleaned and steams removed
1/2 pound chicken white meat, ground
2 ounces goat cheese, room temperature
2 ounces cheddar cheese, grated
1 teaspoon soy sauce
2 tablespoons scallions, finely chopped
1 teaspoon fresh garlic, finely chopped
Sea salt and red pepper, to season

Directions

Pat the mushrooms dry and set them aside.
Thoroughly combine all ingredients, except for the cheddar cheese, in a mixing bowl. Stir to combine well and stuff your mushrooms.
Bake in your Air Fryer at 370 degrees F for 5 minutes. Top with cheddar cheese and continue to cook an additional 3 to 4 minutes or until the cheese melts. Bon appétit!

Turkey Sandwiches

(Ready in about 45 minutes | Servings 4)

427 Calories; 18g Fat; 33.5g Carbs; 32.8g Protein; 6.1g Sugars

Ingredients

1 pound turkey tenderloins
1 tablespoon Dijon-style mustard
1 tablespoon olive oil
Sea salt and ground black pepper, to taste
1 teaspoon Italian seasoning mix
1/4 cup all-purpose flour
1 cup turkey stock
8 slices sourdough, toasted
4 tablespoons tomato ketchup
4 tablespoons mayonnaise
4 pickles, sliced

Directions

Rub the turkey tenderloins with the mustard and olive oil. Season with salt, black pepper, and Italian seasoning mix.

Cook the turkey tenderloins at 350 degrees F for 30 minutes, flipping them over halfway through. Let them rest for 5 to 7 minutes before slicing. For the gravy, in a saucepan, place the drippings from the roasted turkey. Add 1/8 cup of flour and 1/2 cup of turkey stock; whisk until it makes a smooth paste.

Once it gets a golden brown color, add the rest of the stock and flour. Season with salt to taste. Let it simmer over medium heat, stirring constantly for 6 to 7 minutes.

Assemble the sandwiches with the turkey, gravy, tomato ketchup, mayonnaise, and pickles. Serve and enjoy!

Japanese Chicken Teriyaki

(Ready in about 40 minutes | Servings 3)

222 Calories; 4.9g Fat; 3.2g Carbs; 34.1g Protein; 1.1g Sugars

Ingredients

1 pound chicken cutlets
1 teaspoon sesame oil
1 tablespoon lemon juice
1 tablespoon Mirin
1 tablespoon soy sauce
1 teaspoon ginger, peeled and grated
2 garlic cloves, minced
1 teaspoon cornstarch

Directions

Pat dry the chicken cutlets and set them aside.
In a mixing dish, thoroughly combine the remaining ingredients until everything is well incorporated.
Brush the mixture oil over the chicken cutlets and place it in your refrigerator for 30 to 40 minutes.
Cook in the preheated Air Fryer at 360 degrees F for 10 minutes, flipping them halfway through the cooking time. Serve with shirataki noodles and enjoy!

Roasted Sausage and Carrots

(Ready in about 20 minutes | Servings 3)

313 Calories; 13.6g Fat; 14.7g Carbs; 32.3g Protein; 7.2g Sugars

Ingredients

1 pound chicken sausages, smoked
1 pound carrots, trimmed and halved lengthwise
3 tablespoon Dijon mustard
4 tablespoons olive oil
1/2 teaspoon sea salt
1/4 teaspoon ground black pepper

Directions

Start by preheating your Air Fryer to 380 degrees F. Pierce the sausages all over with a fork and add them to the cooking basket. Add the carrots and the remaining ingredients; toss until well coated. Cook for 10 minutes in the preheated Air Fryer. Shake the basket and cook an additional 5 to 7 minutes. Serve warm.

Turkey and Sausage Meatloaf with Herbs

(Ready in about 45 minutes | Servings 4)

431 Calories; 22.3g Fat; 32.6g Carbs; 25.9g Protein; 18.5g Sugars

Ingredients

1/2 cup milk
4 bread slices, crustless
1 tablespoon olive oil
1 onion, finely chopped
1 garlic clove, minced
1/2 pound ground turkey
1/2 pound ground breakfast sausage
1 duck egg, whisked
1 teaspoon rosemary
1 teaspoon basil
1 teaspoon thyme
1 teaspoon cayenne pepper
Kosher salt and ground black pepper, to taste
1/2 cup ketchup
2 tablespoons molasses
1 tablespoon brown mustard

Directions

In a shallow bowl, pour the milk over the bread and let it soak in for 5 to 6 minutes.

Heat 1 tablespoon of oil over medium-high heat in a nonstick pan. Sauté the onions and garlic until tender and fragrant, about 2 minutes.

Add the turkey, sausage, egg, rosemary, basil, thyme, cayenne pepper, salt, and ground black pepper. Stir in the milk-soaked bread. Mix until everything is well incorporated.

Shape the mixture into a loaf and transfer it to a pan that is lightly greased with an olive oil mister.

Next, lower the pan onto the cooking basket.

In a mixing bowl, whisk the ketchup with molasses and mustard. Spread this mixture over the top of your meatloaf.

Cook approximately 27 minutes or until the meatloaf is no longer pink in the middle. Allow it to sit 10 minutes before slicing and serving. Bon appétit!

Chicken-Fajitas with Salsa

(Ready in about 30 minutes | Servings 4)

433 Calories; 14.5g Fat; 44.9g Carbs; 30.2g Protein; 6.6g Sugars

Ingredients

1 pound chicken tenderloins, chopped
Sea salt and ground black pepper, to your liking
1 teaspoon shallot powder
1 teaspoon fajita seasoning
2 bell peppers, seeded and diced
4 flour tortillas
Salsa
1 ancho chili pepper, seeded and finely chopped
2 ripe tomatoes, crushed
1 bunch fresh coriander, roughly chopped
1 lime
2 tablespoons extra-virgin olive oil

Directions

Toss the chicken with salt, pepper, shallot powder, and fajita seasoning mix.
Roast in the preheated Air Fryer at 390 degrees F for 9 minutes. Add the bell peppers and roast an additional 8 minutes.
For the salsa, mix the chilli, tomatoes and coriander. Squeeze over the juice of 1 lime; add olive oil and stir to combine well.
Warm the tortillas in your Air Fryer at 200 degrees F for 10 minutes.
Serve the chicken fajitas with tortilla and salsa. Enjoy!

Marjoram Chicken

(Ready in about 35 minutes | Servings 3)

275 Calories; 12.6g Fat; 14.1g Carbs; 24.3g Protein; 2.9g Sugars

Ingredients

3 chicken drumsticks
Sea salt and ground black pepper, to season
1/2 teaspoon red pepper flakes, crushed
1/2 teaspoon shallot powder
1/2 teaspoon onion powder
1/2 teaspoon garlic powder
1 teaspoon dried marjoram
1/4 cup cornstarch
2 tablespoons balsamic vinegar
2 tablespoons milk

Directions

Pat dry the chicken with paper towels. Toss the chicken drumsticks with all seasonings.

In a shallow bowl, mix the cornstarch, balsamic vinegar and milk until well combined.

Roll the chicken drumsticks onto the cornstarch mixture, pressing to coat well on all sides; shake off any excess pieces of the mixture.

Cook in the preheated Air Fryer at 380 degrees F for 30 minutes, turning them over halfway through the cooking time. Bon appétit!

Chinese Duck

(Ready in about 25 minutes | Servings 3)

512 Calories; 15.4g Fat; 55g Carbs; 38.2g Protein; 11.5g Sugars

Ingredients

2 tablespoons peanuts, chopped
1 tablespoon honey
1 tablespoon olive oil
1 tablespoon hoisin sauce
1 pound duck breast
1 small-sized white onion, sliced
1 teaspoon garlic, chopped
1 celery stick, diced
1 thumb ginger, sliced
4 baby potatoes, diced

Directions

Mix the peanuts, honey, olive oil and hoisin sauce; spread the mixture all over duck breast. Place the duck breast in a lightly oiled cooking basket.

Scatter white onion, garlic, celery, ginger and potatoes over the duck breasts.

Cook in your Air Fryer at 400 degrees F for 20 minutes.

Serve with Mandarin pancakes and enjoy!

Peanut Chicken and Pepper Wraps

(Ready in about 25 minutes | Servings 4)

529 Calories; 25.5g Fat; 31.5g Carbs; 40.1g Protein; 6.8g Sugars

Ingredients

1 ½ pounds chicken breast, boneless and skinless
1/4 cup peanut butter
1 tablespoon sesame oil
1 tablespoon soy sauce
2 teaspoons rice vinegar
1 teaspoon fresh ginger, peeled and grated
1 teaspoon fresh garlic, minced
1 teaspoon brown sugar
2 tablespoons lemon juice, freshly squeezed
4 tortillas
1 bell pepper, julienned

Directions

Start by preheating your Air Fryer to 380 degrees F.
Cook the chicken breasts in the preheated Air Fryer approximately 6 minutes. Turn them over and cook an additional 6 minutes.
Meanwhile, make the sauce by mixing the peanut butter, sesame oil, soy sauce, vinegar, ginger, garlic, sugar, and lemon juice.
Slice the chicken crosswise across the grain into 1/4-inch strips. Toss the chicken into the sauce.
Decrease temperature to 390 degrees F. Spoon the chicken and sauce onto each tortilla; add bell peppers and wrap them tightly. Drizzle with a nonstick cooking spray and bake about 7 minutes. Serve warm.

Double Cheese and Chicken Crescent Bake

(Ready in about 20 minutes | Servings 4)

518 Calories; 25.4g Fat; 38.3g Carbs; 32.7g Protein; 8.6g Sugars

Ingredients

8 ounces regular-sized crescent rolls
1 ½ cups cooked turkey, shredded
1/4 cup prepared warm gravy
1 teaspoon garlic powder
1/4 teaspoon cayenne pepper
Salt and black pepper, to taste
1/2 cup cream of mushroom soup with herbs
1 can milk
1/2 teaspoon freshly ground black pepper
1 cup Colby cheese, shredded
1/4 cup Parmesan cheese grated
2 tablespoons fresh cilantro leaves, roughly chopped

Directions

Start by preheating your Air Fryer to 350 degrees F. Now, spritz the sides and bottom of a baking pan with a nonstick cooking spray.
Roll out the crescent rolls. Top with the turkey and gravy. Sprinkle with the garlic powder, cayenne pepper, salt, and black pepper.
Roll up and arrange them in the prepared baking pan. Mix the soup, milk and 1/2 teaspoon of black pepper to make the sauce. Pour the sauce around the crescents. Top with the cheese.
Bake for 12 minutes or until the top is golden brown. Serve garnished with fresh cilantro leaves. Bon appétit!

Festive Turkey with Chili Mayo

(Ready in about 45 minutes | Servings 4)

409 Calories; 19.2g Fat; 3.4g Carbs; 49.2g Protein; 1.3g Sugars

Ingredients

3 teaspoons olive oil
1/2 teaspoon marjoram
1 teaspoon basil
1/2 teaspoon garlic powder
1 teaspoon shallot powder
Coarse salt and ground black pepper, to taste
2 pounds turkey breast, boneless
Chili mayo:
1/4 cup mayonnaise
1/4 cup sour cream
1 tablespoon chili sauce
1/2 teaspoon stone-ground mustard

Directions

Start by preheating your Air Fryer to 360 degrees F.

In a mixing bowl, thoroughly combine the olive oil with spices. Rub the turkey breast with the spice mixture until it is well coated on all sides.

Air fry for 40 minutes, turning them over halfway through the cooking time. Your instant-read thermometer should read 165 degrees.

Meanwhile, mix all of the ingredients for the chili mayo. Place in your refrigerator until ready to serve.

Place the turkey breast skin-side up on a cutting board and slice it against the grain; serve with chili mayo and enjoy!

Exotic Chicken Drumettes

(Ready in about 25 minutes | Servings 4)

317 Calories; 12.5g Fat; 11.5g Carbs; 38.4g Protein; 10.1g Sugars

Ingredients

1 tablespoons peanut oil
2 tablespoons honey
1 tablespoon tamari sauce
1 tablespoon yellow mustard
1 clove garlic, peeled and minced
2 tablespoons fresh orange juice
1/2 teaspoon sambal oelek
1 ½ pounds chicken drumettes, bone-in
Salt and ground white pepper, to taste
1/4 cup chicken broth
1/2 cup raw onion rings, for garnish

Directions

Start by preheating your Air Fryer to 380 degrees F.
Line the cooking basket with parchment paper. Lightly grease the parchment paper with 1 tablespoon of peanut oil.
In a mixing bowl, thoroughly combine the remaining 1 tablespoon of oil, honey, tamari sauce, mustard, garlic, orange juice, and sambal oelek. Whisk to combine well. Arrange the chicken drumettes in the prepared cooking basket. Season with salt and white pepper.
Spread 1/2 of the honey mixture evenly all over each breast. Pour in the chicken broth. Cook for 12 minutes.
Turn them over, add the remaining 1/2 of the honey mixture, and cook an additional 10 minutes.
Garnish with onion rings and serve immediately.

Thanksgiving Turkey with Mint Sauce

(Ready in about 1 hour | Servings 3)

368 Calories; 11.8g Fat; 11.3g Carbs; 54g Protein; 1.8g Sugars

Ingredients

1 ½ pounds turkey tenderloin
1 teaspoon olive oil
Sea salt and black pepper, to season
1 teaspoon dried thyme
1/2 teaspoon garlic powder
1/2 teaspoon dried sage
Sauce:
2 slices white bread
3/4 ounce fresh mint leaves
1 tablespoon extra-virgin olive oil
1 tablespoon white wine vinegar
1 teaspoon garlic, minced

Directions

Toss the turkey tenderloin with olive oil, salt, pepper, thyme, garlic powder and sage.
Cook in the preheated Air Fryer at 350 degrees F for about 55 minutes, turning it over halfway through the cooking time.
Meanwhile, make the mint sauce; pulse the bread slices in a food processor until coarsely crumbled.
Add in the mint, olive oil, vinegar and garlic; blend again until everything is well incorporated; make sure to add water slowly and gradually until your desired consistency is reached.
Let it rest on a wire rack to cool slightly before carving and serving.
Spoon the sauce over warm turkey and serve. Bon appétit!

Adobo Seasoned Chicken with Veggies

(Ready in about 1 hour 30 minutes | Servings 4)

427 Calories; 15.3g Fat; 18.5g Carbs; 52.3g Protein; 9.4g Sugars

Ingredients

2 pounds chicken wings, rinsed and patted dry
1 teaspoon coarse sea salt
1/4 teaspoon ground black pepper
1/2 teaspoon red pepper flakes, crushed
1 teaspoon ground cumin
1 teaspoon paprika
1 teaspoon granulated onion
1 teaspoon ground turmeric
2 tablespoons tomato powder
1 tablespoon dry Madeira wine
2 stalks celery, diced
2 cloves garlic, peeled but not chopped
1 large Spanish onion, diced
2 bell peppers, seeded and sliced
4 carrots, trimmed and halved
2 tablespoons olive oil

Directions

Toss all ingredients in a large bowl. Cover and let it sit for 1 hour in your refrigerator.
Add the chicken wings to a baking pan.
Roast the chicken wings in the preheated Air Fryer at 380 degrees F for 7 minutes.
Add the vegetables and cook an additional 15 minutes, shaking the basket once or twice. Serve warm.

Paprika Chicken Legs with Brussels Sprouts

(Ready in about 30 minutes | Servings 2)

355 Calories; 20.1g Fat; 5.3g Carbs; 36.6g Protein; 0.2g Sugars

Ingredients

2 chicken legs
1/2 teaspoon paprika
1/2 teaspoon kosher salt
1/2 teaspoon black pepper
1 pound Brussels sprouts
1 teaspoon dill, fresh or dried

Directions

Start by preheating your Air Fryer to 370 degrees F.
Now, season your chicken with paprika, salt, and pepper. Transfer the chicken legs to the cooking basket. Cook for 10 minutes.
Flip the chicken legs and cook an additional 10 minutes. Reserve.
Add the Brussels sprouts to the cooking basket; sprinkle with dill. Cook at 380 degrees F for 15 minutes, shaking the basket halfway through.
Serve with the reserved chicken legs. Bon appétit!

Roast Turkey

(Ready in about 50 minutes | Servings 6)

316 Calories; 24.2g Fat; 2.5g Carbs; 20.4g Protein; 1.1g Sugars

Ingredients

1 pounds turkey
1 tablespoon fresh rosemary, chopped
1 teaspoon sea salt
1/2 teaspoon ground black pepper
1 onion, chopped
1 celery stalk, chopped

Directions

Start by preheating your Air Fryer to 360 degrees F. Spritz the sides and bottom of the cooking basket with a nonstick cooking spray. Place the turkey in the cooking basket. Add the rosemary, salt, and black pepper. Cook for 30 minutes in the preheated Air Fryer. Add the onion and celery and cook an additional 15 minutes. Bon appétit!

Italian Chicken and Cheese Frittata

(Ready in about 25 minutes | Servings 4)

329 Calories; 25.3g Fat; 3.4g Carbs; 21.1g Protein; 2.3g Sugars

Ingredients

1 (1-pound) fillet chicken breast
Sea salt and ground black pepper, to taste
1 tablespoon olive oil
4 eggs
1/2 teaspoon cayenne pepper
1/2 cup Mascarpone cream
1/4 cup Asiago cheese, freshly grated

Directions

Flatten the chicken breast with a meat mallet. Season with salt and pepper.

Heat the olive oil in a frying pan over medium flame. Cook the chicken for 10 to 12 minutes; slice into small strips, and reserve.

Then, in a mixing bowl, thoroughly combine the eggs, and cayenne pepper; season with salt to taste. Add the cheese and stir to combine. Add the reserved chicken. Then, pour the mixture into a lightly greased pan; put the pan into the cooking basket.

Cook in the preheated Air Fryer at 355 degrees F for 10 minutes, flipping over halfway through.

Pork

Honey Roasted Pork Tenderloin

(Ready in about 20 minutes + marinating time | Servings 3)

231 Calories; 3.6g Fat; 15.3g Carbs; 32.2g Protein; 13.4g Sugars

Ingredients

1 garlic clove, pressed
2 tablespoons honey
2 tablespoons Worcestershire sauce
2 tablespoons tequila
2 tablespoons yellow mustard
1 pound pork tenderloin, sliced into 3 pieces
1 teaspoon rosemary
1 teaspoon basil
1/2 teaspoon oregano
1/2 teaspoon parsley flakes
Salt and black pepper, to taste

Directions

In a glass bowl, thoroughly combine the garlic, honey, Worcestershire sauce, tequila and mustard.
Add in the pork tenderloin pieces, cover and marinate in your refrigerator for about 1 hour.
Transfer the pork tenderloin to the cooking basket, discarding the marinade. Sprinkle the pork tenderloin with herbs, salt and black pepper.
Cook in your Air Fryer at 370 degrees F for 15 minutes, checking periodically and basting with the reserved marinade. Serve warm.

Pork & Parmesan Meatballs

(Ready in about 15 minutes | Servings 3)

539 Calories; 38.4g Fat; 17.5g Carbs; 29.2g Protein; 4.3g Sugars

Ingredients

1 pound ground pork
2 tablespoons tamari sauce
1 teaspoon garlic, minced
2 tablespoons spring onions, finely chopped
1 tablespoon brown sugar
1 tablespoon olive oil
1/2 cup breadcrumbs
2 tablespoons parmesan cheese, preferably freshly grated

Directions

Combine the ground pork, tamari sauce, garlic, onions, and sugar in a mixing dish. Mix until everything is well incorporated.
Form the mixture into small meatballs.
In a shallow bowl, mix the olive oil, breadcrumbs, and parmesan.
Roll the meatballs over the parmesan mixture.
Cook at 380 degrees F for 3 minutes; shake the basket and cook an additional 4 minutes or until meatballs are browned on all sides. Bon appétit!

Boston Butt with Salsa Verde

(Ready in about 35 minutes | Servings 4)

374 Calories; 24.1g Fat; 8.6g Carbs; 29.9g Protein; 4.7g Sugars

Ingredients

1 pound Boston butt, thinly sliced across the grain into 2-inch-long strips
1/2 teaspoon red pepper flakes, crushed
Sea salt and ground black pepper, to taste
1/2 pound tomatillos, chopped
1 small-sized onion, chopped
2 chili peppers, chopped
2 cloves garlic
2 tablespoons fresh cilantro, chopped
1 tablespoon olive oil
1 teaspoon sea salt

Directions

Rub the Boston butt with red pepper, salt, and black pepper. Spritz the bottom of the cooking basket with a nonstick cooking spray.
Roast the Boston butt in the preheated Air Fryer at 390 degrees F for 10 minutes. Shake the basket and cook another 10 minutes.
While the pork is roasting, make the salsa.
Blend the remaining ingredients until smooth and uniform. Transfer the mixture to a saucepan and add 1 cup of water.
Bring to a boil; reduce the heat and simmer for 8 to 12 minutes.
Serve the roasted pork with the salsa verde on the side. Enjoy!

Pork Cutlets with Pearl Onions

(Ready in about 20 minutes | Servings 2)

292 Calories; 6.4g Fat; 20.3g Carbs; 36.4g Protein; 3.7g Sugars

Ingredients

2 pork cutlets
1 teaspoon onion powder
1/2 teaspoon cayenne pepper
Sea salt and black pepper, to taste
1/4 cup flour
1/4 cup Pecorino Romano cheese, grated
1 cup pearl onions

Directions

Toss the pork cutlets with the onion powder, cayenne pepper, salt, black pepper, flour and cheese.
Transfer the pork cutlets to the lightly oiled cooking basket. Scatter pearl onions around the pork.
Cook in the preheated Air Fryer at 360 degrees for 15 minutes, turning over halfway through the cooking time.
Bon appétit!

Blade Steaks with Broccoli

(Ready in about 30 minutes | Servings 4)

443 Calories; 29.5g Fat; 11.3g Carbs; 34.2g Protein; 2.8g Sugars

Ingredients

1 ½ pounds blade steaks skinless, boneless
Kosher salt and ground black pepper, to taste
2 garlic cloves, crushed
2 tablespoons soy sauce
1 tablespoon oyster sauce
2 tablespoon lemon juice
1 pound broccoli, broken into florets
2 tablespoons butter, melted
1 teaspoon dried dill weed
2 tablespoons sunflower seeds, lightly toasted

Directions

Start by preheating your Air Fryer to 385 degrees F. Spritz the bottom and sides of the cooking basket with cooking spray.
Now, season the pork with salt and black pepper. Add the garlic, soy sauce, oyster sauce, and lemon juice.
Cook for 20 minutes; turning over halfway through the cooking time.
Toss the broccoli with the melted butter and dill. Add the broccoli to the cooking basket and cook at 400 degrees F for 6 minutes, shaking the basket periodically.
Serve the warm pork with broccoli and garnish with sunflower seeds. Bon appétit!

Pork Pot Stickers

(Ready in about 10 minutes | Servings 2)

352 Calories; 13.5g Fat; 27.8g Carbs; 31.2g Protein; 2.2g Sugars

Ingredients

1/2 pound lean ground pork
1/2 teaspoon fresh ginger, freshly grated
1 teaspoon chili garlic sauce
1 tablespoon soy sauce
1 tablespoon rice wine
1/4 teaspoon Szechuan pepper
2 stalks scallions, chopped
1 tablespoon sesame oil
8 (3-inch) round wonton wrappers

Directions

Cook the ground pork in a preheated skillet until no longer pink, crumbling with a fork. Stir in the other ingredients, except for the wonton wrappers; stir to combine well.

Place the wonton wrappers on a clean work surface. Divide the pork filling between the wrappers. Wet the edge of each wrapper with water, fold the top half over the bottom half and pinch the border to seal.

Place the pot stickers in the cooking basket and brush them with a little bit of olive oil. Cook the pot sticker at 400 degrees F for 8 minutes. Serve immediately.

Pork Shoulder with Molasses Sauce

(Ready in about 25 minutes + marinating time | Servings 3)

353 Calories; 19.6g Fat; 13.5g Carbs; 29.2g Protein; 12.2g Sugars

Ingredients

2 tablespoons molasses
2 tablespoons soy sauce
2 tablespoons Shaoxing wine
2 garlic cloves, minced
1 teaspoon fresh ginger, minced
1 tablespoon cilantro stems and leaves, finely chopped
1 pound boneless pork shoulder
2 tablespoons sesame oil

Directions

In a large-sized ceramic dish, thoroughly combine the molasses, soy sauce, wine, garlic, ginger, and cilantro; add the pork shoulder and allow it to marinate for 2 hours in the refrigerator.
Then, grease the cooking basket with sesame oil. Place the pork shoulder in the cooking basket; reserve the marinade.
Cook in the preheated Air Fryer at 395 degrees F for 14 to 17 minutes, flipping and basting with the marinade halfway through. Let it rest for 5 to 6 minutes before slicing and serving.
While the pork is roasting, cook the marinade in a preheated skillet over medium heat; cook until it has thickened.
Brush the pork shoulder with the sauce and enjoy!

Sausage and Mushroom Chili

(Ready in about 35 minutes | Servings 4)

569 Calories; 35.3g Fat; 33.1g Carbs; 33.1g Protein; 10.4g Sugars

Ingredients

1 tablespoon olive oil
1 shallot, chopped
2 garlic cloves, smashed
10 ounces button mushrooms, sliced
1/2 pound pork sausages, chopped
2 cups tomato puree
2 tablespoons tomato ketchup
1 teaspoon yellow mustard
1 cup chicken broth
2 teaspoons ancho chili powder
Salt and ground black pepper, to taste
1 (16-ounce) can pinto beans, rinsed and drained
1/2 cup cream cheese

Directions

Start by preheating your Air Fryer to 360 degrees F. Heat the oil in a baking pan for a few minutes and cook the shallot until tender about 4 minutes.

Add the garlic and mushrooms; cook another 4 minutes or until tender and fragrant.

Next, stir in sausage and cook for a further 9 minutes. Add tomato puree, ketchup, mustard, and broth. Stir to combine and cook another 6 minutes.

Add spices and beans; cook an additional 7 minutes. Divide between individual bowls and top each bowl with cream cheese. Enjoy!

Ribs with Cherry Tomatoes

(Ready in about 35 minutes | Servings 2)

452 Calories; 17.1g Fat; 17.7g Carbs; 55.2g Protein; 13.6g Sugars

Ingredients

1 rack ribs, cut in half to fit the Air Fryer
1/4 cup dry white wine
2 tablespoons soy sauce
1 tablespoon Dijon mustard
Sea salt and ground black pepper, to taste
1 cup cherry tomatoes
1 teaspoon dried rosemary

Directions

Toss the pork ribs with wine, soy sauce, mustard, salt, and black pepper.
Add the ribs to the lightly greased cooking basket. Cook in the preheated Air Fryer at 370 degrees F for 25 minutes.
Turn the ribs over, add the cherry tomatoes and rosemary; cook an additional 5 minutes. Serve immediately.

Meatballs with Sweet and Sour Sauce

(Ready in about 20 minutes | Servings 3)

486 Calories; 14.8g Fat; 54.1g Carbs; 33.6g Protein; 20.4g Sugars

Ingredients

Meatballs:
1/2 pound ground pork
1/4 pound ground turkey
1 tablespoons scallions, minced
1/2 teaspoon garlic, minced
4 tablespoons tortilla chips, crushed
4 tablespoons parmesan cheese, grated
1 egg, beaten
Salt and red pepper, to taste Sauce:
6 ounces jellied cranberry
2 ounces hot sauce
2 tablespoons molasses
1 tablespoon wine vinegar

Directions

In a mixing bowl, thoroughly combine all ingredients for the meatballs. Stir to combine well and roll the mixture into 8 equal meatballs.
Cook in the preheated Air Fryer at 400 degrees F for 7 minutes. Shake the basket and continue to cook for 7 minutes longer.
Meanwhile, whisk the sauce ingredients in a nonstick skillet over low heat; let it simmer, partially covered, for about 20 minutes. Fold in the prepared meatballs and serve immediately.
Bon appétit!

Pork Tenderloin with Brussels Sprouts

(Ready in about 20 minutes | Servings 3)

381 Calories; 11.7g Fat; 14.1g Carbs; 56g Protein; 3.4g Sugars

Ingredients

1 pound Brussels sprouts, halved
1 ½ pounds tenderloin
1 teaspoon peanut oil
1 teaspoon garlic powder
1 tablespoon coriander, minced
2 teaspoon smoked paprika
Sea salt and ground black pepper, to taste

Directions

Toss the Brussels sprouts and pork with oil and spices until well coated.
Place in the Air Fryer cooking basket. Cook in the preheated Air Fryer at 370 degrees F for 15 minutes.
Taste and adjust seasonings. Eat warm.

Spaghetti Bolognese

(Ready in about 30 minutes | Servings 4)

551 Calories; 25.9g Fat; 50.1g Carbs; 29.1g Protein; 5.5g Sugars

Ingredients

2 tablespoons olive oil
1 shallot, peeled and chopped
1 teaspoon fresh garlic, minced
1 pound lean ground pork
1 cup tomato puree
2 tablespoons apple cider vinegar
1 teaspoon oregano
1 teaspoon basil
1 teaspoon rosemary
Salt and black pepper, to taste
1 package spaghetti
1 tablespoon fresh parsley

Directions

Heat the oil in a baking pan at 380 degrees F. Then, sauté the shallots until tender about 4 minutes.
Add the garlic and ground pork; cook an additional 6 minutes, stirring and crumbling meat with a spatula.
Add the tomato puree, vinegar, and spices; cook for 4 to 6 minutes longer or until everything is heated through.
Meanwhile, bring a large pot of lightly salted water to a boil. Cook your spaghetti for 10 to 12 minutes; drain and divide between individual plates.
Top with the Bolognese sauce and serve garnished with fresh parsley. Bon appétit!

Pork Fillets with Apples

(Ready in about 20 minutes | Servings 3)

485 Calories; 27.3g Fat; 14.7g Carbs; 42.8g Protein; 7.1g Sugars

Ingredients

1/4 cup chickpea flour
2 tablespoons Romano cheese, grated
1 teaspoon onion powder
1 teaspoon garlic powder
1/2 teaspoon ground cumin
1 teaspoon cayenne pepper
2 pork fillets (1 pound)
1 Granny Smiths apple, peeled and sliced
1 tablespoon lemon juice
1 ounce butter, cold

Directions

Combine the flour, cheese, onions powder, garlic powder, cumin, and cayenne pepper in a ziploc bag; shake to mix well.
Place the pork fillets in the bag. Shake to coat on all sides. Next, spritz the bottom of the Air Fryer basket with cooking spray.
Cook in the preheated Air Fryer at 370 degrees F for 10 minutes.
Add the apples and drizzle with lemon juice; place the cold butter on top and cook an additional 5 minutes. Serve immediately.

Keto Crispy Pork Chops

(Ready in about 20 minutes | Servings 3)

467 Calories; 26.8g Fat; 2.7g Carbs; 50.3g Protein; 1.3g Sugars

Ingredients

2 center-cut pork chops, boneless
1/2 teaspoon paprika
Sea salt and ground black pepper, to taste
1/4 cup Romano cheese, grated
1/4 cup crushed pork rinds
1/2 teaspoon garlic powder
1/2 teaspoon mustard seeds
1/2 teaspoon dried marjoram
1 egg, beaten
1 tablespoon buttermilk
1 teaspoon peanut oil

Directions

Pat the pork chops dry with kitchen towels. Season them with paprika, salt and black pepper.
Add the Romano cheese, crushed pork rinds, garlic powder, mustard seeds and marjoram to a rimmed plate.
Beat the egg and buttermilk in another plate. Now, dip the pork chops in the egg, then in the cheese/pork rind mixture.

Drizzle the pork with peanut oil. Cook in the preheated Air Fryer at 400 degrees F for 12 minutes, flipping pork chops halfway through the cooking time.
Serve with keto-friendly sides such as cauliflower rice. Bon appétit!

Party Pork and Bacon Skewers

(Ready in about 30 minutes + marinating time | Servings 6)

572 Calories; 41.1g Fat; 8.9g Carbs; 41.6g Protein; 5.4g Sugars

Ingredients

1 cup cream of celery soup
1 (13.5-ounce) can coconut milk, unsweetened
2 tablespoons tamari sauce
1 teaspoon yellow mustard
1 tablespoon honey
Salt and freshly ground white pepper, to taste
1/2 teaspoon cayenne pepper
1/2 teaspoon chili powder
1 teaspoon curry powder
2 pounds pork tenderloin, cut into bite-sized cubes
4 ounces bacon, cut into pieces
12 bamboo skewers, soaked in water

Directions

In a large pot, bring the cream of the celery soup, coconut milk, tamari sauce, mustard, honey, salt, white pepper, cayenne pepper, chili powder, and curry powder to a boil. Then, reduce the heat to simmer; cook until the sauce is heated through, about 13 minutes. Add the pork, gently stir, and place in your refrigerator for 2 hours. Thread the pork onto the skewers, alternating the cubes of meat with the pieces of bacon. Preheat your Air Fryer to 370 degrees F. Cook for 15 minutes, turning over a couple of times. Bon appétit!

Bacon with Onions Rings and Remoulade Sauce

(Ready in about 15 minutes | Servings 2)

371 Calories; 32.7g Fat; 11.2g Carbs; 8.5g Protein; 5.3g Sugars

Ingredients

1 thick bacon slices
8 ounces onion rings, frozen
1 teaspoon yellow mustard
2 tablespoons mayonnaise
1/4 teaspoon paprika
1 teaspoon hot sauce
Salt and black pepper, to taste

Directions

Place the slices of bacon and onion rings in the Air Fryer cooking basket.
Cook the bacon and onion rings at 400 degrees F for 4 minutes; shake the basket and cook for a further 4 minutes or until cooked through.
Meanwhile, make the Remoulade sauce by whisking the remaining ingredients. Arrange the bacon and onion rings on plates and garnish with Remoulade sauce. Bon appétit!

Italian Sausage Meatball Casserole

(Ready in about 35 minutes | Servings 4)

534 Calories; 29.7g Fat; 46g Carbs; 23.1g Protein; 8.1g Sugars

Ingredients

1 pound Italian pork sausage, crumbled
1 egg
1 cup regular rolled oat
1 teaspoon cayenne pepper
Sea salt and ground black pepper, to taste
1 tablespoon olive oil
1 leek, chopped
1 teaspoon fresh garlic, minced
1 chili pepper, chopped
1 teaspoon dried oregano
1 teaspoon dried basil
1 teaspoon celery seeds
1 teaspoon brown mustard
2 cups tomato puree

Directions

In a mixing bowl, thoroughly combine the pork sausage with egg, oats, cayenne pepper, salt, and black pepper. Form the sausage mixture into meatballs.

Spritz the Air Fryer basket with cooking oil. Cook the meatballs in the preheated Air Fryer at 380 degrees for 10 minutes, shaking the basket halfway through the cooking time. Reserve.

Meanwhile, heat the olive oil in a pan over medium-high heat. Sauté the leeks until tender and aromatic.

Stir in the garlic, pepper, and seasonings and cook for a further 2 minutes. Add the brown mustard and tomato puree and cook another 5 minutes.

Transfer the tomato sauce to the baking pan. Add the meatballs and cook in the preheated Air Fryer at 350 degrees F for 10 minutes. Serve warm.

Chinese Char Siu Pork

(Ready in about 25 minutes + marinating time | Servings 3)

246 Calories; 10.3g Fat; 7.8g Carbs; 28.6g Protein; 6.7g Sugars

Ingredients

1 pound pork shoulder, cut into long strips
1/2 teaspoon Chinese five-spice powder
1/4 teaspoon Szechuan pepper
1 tablespoon hoisin sauce
2 tablespoons hot water
1 teaspoon sesame oil
1 tablespoon Shaoxing wine
1 tablespoon molasses

Directions

Place all ingredients in a ceramic dish and let it marinate for 2 hours in the refrigerator.
Cook in the preheated Air Fryer at 390 degrees F for 20 minutes, shaking the basket halfway through the cooking time.
Heat the reserved marinade in a wok for about 15 minutes or until the sauce has thickened.
Spoon the sauce over the warm pork shoulder and serve with rice if desired. Enjoy!

Pork Leg with Candy Onions

(Ready in about 1 hour | Servings 4)

444 Calories; 12.8g Fat; 11.6g Carbs; 67g Protein; 6.8g Sugars

Ingredients

1 rosemary sprig, chopped
1 thyme sprig, chopped
1 teaspoon dried sage, crushed
Sea salt and ground black pepper, to taste
1 teaspoon cayenne pepper
2 teaspoons sesame oil
2 pounds pork leg roast, scored
1 pound candy onions, peeled
2 chili peppers, minced
4 cloves garlic, finely chopped

Directions

Start by preheating your Air Fryer to 400 degrees F.
Then, mix the seasonings with the sesame oil.
Rub the seasoning mixture all over the pork leg. Cook in the preheated Air Fryer for 40 minutes.
Add the candy onions, peppers and garlic and cook an additional 12 minutes. Slice the pork leg.
Afterwards, spoon the pan juices over the meat and serve with the candy onions. Bon appétit!

Ground Pork and Wild Rice Casserole

(Ready in about 25 minutes | Servings 3)

506 Calories; 34.7g Fat; 13.4g Carbs; 34.7g Protein; 2.3g Sugars

Ingredients

1 teaspoon olive oil
1 small-sized yellow onion, chopped
1 pound ground pork (84% lean)
Salt and black pepper, to taste
1/2 cups cooked wild rice, uncooked
1/2 cup cream of mushroom soup
1/2 tomato paste
1 jalapeno pepper, minced
1 teaspoon Italian spice mix
1/2 cup Asiago cheese, shredded

Directions

Start by preheating your Air Fryer to 350 degrees F.
Heat the olive oil in a nonstick over medium-high heat. Then, sauté the onion and ground pork for 6 to 7 minutes, crumbling with a spatula. Season with salt and black pepper to your liking.
Spoon the pork mixture into a lightly greased baking dish.
Spoon the cooked rice over the pork layer. In a mixing dish, thoroughly combine the remaining ingredients.
Bake for 15 minutes or until bubbly and heated through. Bon appétit!

Herb-Crusted Pork Roast

(Ready in about 1 hour | Servings 2)

220 Calories; 11.4g Fat; 3.3g Carbs; 24.9g Protein; 1.7g Sugars

Ingredients

1/2 pound pork loin
Salt and black pepper, to taste
1/2 teaspoon onion powder
1/2 teaspoon parsley flakes
1/2 teaspoon oregano
1/2 teaspoon thyme
1/2 teaspoon grated lemon peel
1 teaspoon garlic, minced
1 teaspoon butter, softened

Directions

Pat the pork loin dry with kitchen towels. Season it with salt and black pepper.
In a bowl, mix the remaining ingredients until well combined.
Coat the pork with the herb rub, pressing to adhere well.
Cook in the preheated Air Fryer at 360 degrees F for 30 minutes; turn it over and cook on the other side for 25 minutes more. Bon appétit!

Omelet with Prosciutto and Ricotta Cheese

(Ready in about 15 minutes | Servings 2)

389 Calories; 28.8g Fat; 3.2g Carbs; 29.1g Protein; 0.5g Sugars

Ingredients

2 tablespoons olive oil
4 eggs
2 tablespoons scallions, chopped
4 tablespoons Ricotta cheese
1/4 teaspoon black pepper, freshly cracked
Salt, to taste
6 ounces prosciutto, chopped
1 tablespoon Italian parsley, roughly chopped

Directions

Generously grease a baking pan with olive oil.
Then, whisk the eggs, and add the scallions, cheese, black pepper, and salt. Fold in the chopped prosciutto and mix to combine well. Spoon into the prepared baking pan.
Cook in the preheated Air Fryer at 360 F for 6 minutes. Serve immediately garnished with Italian parsley.

Warm Pork Salad

(Ready in about 20 minutes | Servings 3)

315 Calories; 13.3g Fat; 15.5g Carbs; 30.5g Protein; 10.2g Sugars

Ingredients

1 pound pork shoulder, cut into strips
1/4 teaspoon fresh ginger, minced
1 teaspoon garlic, pressed
1 tablespoon olive oil
1 tablespoon honey
2 teaspoons fresh cilantro, chopped
1 tablespoon Worcestershire sauce
1 medium-sized cucumber, sliced
1 cup arugula
1 cup baby spinach
1 cup Romaine lettuce
1 tomato, diced
1 shallot, sliced

Directions

Spritz the Air Fryer cooking basket with a nonstick spray. Place the pork in the Air Fryer cooking basket.
Cook at 400 degrees F for 13 minutes, shaking the basket halfway through the cooking time.
Transfer the meat to a serving bowl and toss with the remaining ingredients.
Bon appétit!

Mexican-Style Ground Pork with Peppers

(Ready in about 40 minutes | Servings 4)

505 Calories; 39.4g Fat; 9.9g Carbs; 28g Protein; 5.1g Sugars

Ingredients

2 chili peppers
1 red bell pepper
2 tablespoons olive oil
1 large-sized shallot, chopped
1 pound ground pork
2 garlic cloves, minced
2 ripe tomatoes, pureed
1 teaspoon dried marjoram
1/2 teaspoon mustard seeds
1/2 teaspoon celery seeds
1 teaspoon Mexican oregano
1 tablespoon fish sauce
2 tablespoons fresh coriander, chopped
Salt and ground black pepper, to taste
2 cups water
1 tablespoon chicken bouillon granules
2 tablespoons sherry wine
1 cup Mexican cheese blend

Directions

Roast the peppers in the preheated Air Fryer at 395 degrees F for 10 minutes, flipping them halfway through cook time.

Let them steam for 10 minutes; then, peel the skin and discard the stems and seeds. Slice the peppers into halves.

Heat the olive oil in a baking pan at 380 degrees F for 2 minutes; add the shallots and cook for 4 minutes. Add the ground pork and garlic; cook for a further 4 to 5 minutes.

After that, stir in the tomatoes, marjoram, mustard seeds, celery seeds, oregano, fish sauce, coriander, salt, and pepper. Add a layer of sliced peppers to the baking pan.

Mix the water with the chicken bouillon granules and sherry wine. Add the mixture to the baking pan.

Cook in the preheated Air Fryer at 395 degrees F for 10 minutes. Top with cheese and bake an additional 5 minutes until the cheese has melted. Serve immediately.

Taco Casserole with Cheese

(Ready in about 25 minutes | Servings 4)

449 Calories; 23g Fat; 5.6g Carbs; 54g Protein; 3.2g Sugars

Ingredients

1 pound lean ground pork
1/2 pound ground beef
1/4 cup tomato puree
Sea salt and ground black pepper, to taste
1 teaspoon smoked paprika
1/2 teaspoon dried oregano
1 teaspoon dried basil
1 teaspoon dried rosemary
2 eggs
1 cup Cottage cheese, crumbled, at room temperature
1/2 cup Cotija cheese, shredded

Directions

Lightly grease a casserole dish with a nonstick cooking oil. Add the ground meat to the bottom of your casserole dish.

Add the tomato puree. Sprinkle with salt, black pepper, paprika, oregano, basil, and rosemary.

In a mixing bowl, whisk the egg with cheese. Place on top of the ground meat mixture. Place a piece of foil on top.

Bake in the preheated Air Fryer at 350 degrees F for 10 minutes; remove the foil and cook an additional 6 minutes. Bon appétit!

Beef

Greek-Style Roast Beef

(Ready in about 55 minutes | Servings 3)

348 Calories; 16.1g Fat; 1.6g Carbs; 49g Protein; 0.9g Sugars

Ingredients

1 clove garlic, halved
1 ½ pounds beef eye round roast
1 zucchini, sliced lengthwise
2 teaspoons olive oil
1 teaspoon Greek spice mix
Sea salt, to season
1/2 cup Greek-style yogurt

Directions

Rub the beef eye round roast with garlic halves.
Brush the beef eye round roast and zucchini with olive oil. Sprinkle with spices and place the beef in the cooking basket.
Roast in your Air Fryer at 400 degrees F for 40 minutes. Turn the beef over.
Add the zucchini to the cooking basket and continue to cook for 12 minutes more or until cooked through. Serve warm, garnished with Greek-style yogurt. Enjoy!

Cheesy Meatballs

(Ready in about 15 minutes | Servings 4)

613 Calories; 35.1g Fat; 16.1g Carbs; 57g Protein; 2g Sugars

Ingredients

1 pound ground beef
1/4 cup Grana Padano, grated
2 tablespoons scallion, chopped
2 garlic cloves, minced
2 stale crustless bread slices
1 tablespoon Italian seasoning mix
1 egg, beaten
1/4 cup Mozzarella cheese, shredded
Kosher salt and ground black pepper, to taste

Directions

In a mixing bowl, combine all ingredients. Then, shape the mixture into 8 meatballs.
Cook the meatballs at 370 degrees F for 10 minutes, shaking the basket halfway through the cooking time.
Serve the meatballs in a sandwich if desired.

Roasted Ribeye with Mayo

(Ready in about 20 minutes | Servings 3)

437 Calories; 24.8g Fat; 1.8g Carbs; 51g Protein; 0.1g Sugars

Ingredients

1 ½ pounds ribeye, bone-in
1 tablespoon butter, room temperature
Salt, to taste
1/2 teaspoon crushed black pepper
1/2 teaspoon dried dill
1/2 teaspoon cayenne pepper
1/2 teaspoon garlic powder
1/2 teaspoon onion powder
1 teaspoon ground coriander
3 tablespoons mayonnaise
1 teaspoon garlic, minced

Directions

Start by preheating your Air Fryer to 400 degrees F.
Pat dry the ribeye and rub it with softened butter on all sides.
Sprinkle with seasonings and transfer to the cooking basket.
Cook in the preheated Air Fryer for 15 minutes, flipping them halfway through the cooking time.
In the meantime, simply mix the mayonnaise with garlic and place in the refrigerator until ready to serve. Bon appétit!

Sausage and Veggie Sandwiches

(Ready in about 35 minutes | Servings 4)

627 Calories; 41.9g Fat; 41.3g Carbs; 22.2g Protein; 9.3g Sugars

Ingredients

4 bell peppers
2 tablespoons canola oil
4 medium-sized tomatoes, halved
4 spring onions
4 beef sausages
4 hot dog buns
1 tablespoon mustard

Directions

Start by preheating your Air Fryer to 400 degrees F.
Add the bell peppers to the cooking basket. Drizzle 1 tablespoon of canola oil all over the bell peppers.
Cook for 5 minutes. Turn the temperature down to 350 degrees F.
Add the tomatoes and spring onions to the cooking basket and cook an additional 10 minutes.
Reserve your vegetables.
Then, add the sausages to the cooking basket. Drizzle with the remaining tablespoon of canola oil.
Cook in the preheated Air Fryer at 380 degrees F for 15 minutes, flipping them halfway through the cooking time.
Add the sausage to a hot dog bun; top with the air-fried vegetables and mustard; serve.

Kansas City-Style Ribs

(Ready in about 35 minutes + marinating time | Servings 3)

327 Calories; 13.4g Fat; 9.2g Carbs; 32.4g Protein; 6.9g Sugars

Ingredients

1 pound beef ribs
1/4 cup ketchup
1/4 cup rum
1 tablespoon mustard
1 tablespoon olive oil
1 tablespoon brown sugar
1 teaspoon garlic powder
1/2 teaspoon onion powder
1/2 teaspoon chili powder
1 teaspoon liquid smoke
Sea salt and ground black pepper, to season

Directions

Place all ingredients in a ceramic bowl, cover and allow it to marinate for 3 to 4 hours.
Roast in your Air Fryer at 400 degrees F for 10 minutes. Reduce heat to 330 degrees F and cook an additional 20 minutes.
Warm the remaining marinade in a nonstick skillet over a moderate flame to make the sauce.
Drizzle the sauce over the beef ribs and eat warm.

Mayo Roasted Sirloin Steak

(Ready in about 20 minutes | Servings 3)

418 Calories; 31.3g Fat; 0.2g Carbs; 30.1g Protein; 0.2g Sugars

Ingredients

1 pound sirloin steak, cubed
1/2 cup mayonnaise
1 tablespoon red wine vinegar
1/2 teaspoon dried basil
1 teaspoon garlic, minced
1/2 teaspoon cayenne pepper
Kosher salt and ground black pepper, to season

Directions

Pat dry the sirloin steak with paper towels.
In a small mixing dish, thoroughly combine the remaining ingredients until everything is well incorporated.
Toss the cubed steak with the mayonnaise mixture and transfer to the Air Fryer cooking basket.
Cook in the preheated Air Fryer at 400 degrees F for 7 minutes. Shake the basket and continue to cook for a further 7 minutes. Bon appétit!

Meatballs with Cranberry Sauce

(Ready in about 40 minutes | Servings 4)

520 Calories; 22.4g Fat; 44g Carbs; 45.4g Protein; 25.5g Sugars

Ingredients

Meatballs:
1 ½ pounds ground chuck
1 egg
1 cup rolled oats
1/2 cup Romano cheese, grated
1/2 teaspoon dried basil
1/2 teaspoon dried oregano
1 teaspoon paprika
2 garlic cloves, minced
2 tablespoons scallions, chopped
Sea salt and cracked black pepper, to taste
Cranberry Sauce:
10 ounces BBQ sauce
8 ounces cranberry sauce

Directions

In a large bowl, mix all ingredients for the meatballs. Mix until everything is well incorporated; then, shape the meat mixture into 2-inch balls using a cookie scoop. Transfer them to the lightly greased cooking basket and cook at 380 degrees F for 10 minutes. Shake the basket occasionally and work in batches. Add the BBQ sauce and cranberry sauce to a saucepan and cook over moderate heat until you achieve a glaze-like consistency; it will take about 15 minutes.
Gently stir in the air fried meatballs and cook an additional 3 minutes or until heated through. Enjoy

Chuck Roast with Sweet 'n' Sticky Sauce

(Ready in about 35 minutes | Servings 3)

325 Calories; 16.8g Fat; 13.7g Carbs; 31.9g Protein; 12.8g Sugars

Ingredients

1 pound chuck roast
Sea salt and ground black pepper, to taste
2 tablespoons butter, softened
1 tablespoon coriander, chopped
1 tablespoon fresh scallions, chopped
1 teaspoon soy sauce
1 tablespoon fish sauce
2 tablespoons honey

Directions

Season the chuck roast with salt and pepper; spritz a nonstick cooking oil all over the beef.
Air fry at 400 degrees F for 30 to 35 minutes, flipping the chuck roast halfway through the cooking time.
While the roast is cooking, heat the other ingredients in a sauté pan over medium-high heat. Bring to a boil and reduce the heat; let it simmer, partially covered, until the sauce has thickened and reduced.
Slice the chuck roast into thick cuts and serve garnished with sweet 'n' sticky sauce. Bon appétit!

Moroccan-Style Steak Salad

(Ready in about 20 minutes | Servings 4)

522 Calories; 21.7g Fat; 28.2g Carbs; 51.3g Protein; 13.5g Sugars

Ingredients

1 pounds flank steak
1/4 cup soy sauce
4 tablespoons dry red wine
Salt, to taste
1/2 teaspoon ground black pepper
2 parsnips, peeled and sliced lengthways
1 teaspoon paprika
1 teaspoon onion powder
1 teaspoon garlic powder
1/2 teaspoon ground coriander
1/4 teaspoon ground allspice
2 tablespoons olive oil
2 tablespoons lime juice
1 teaspoon honey
1 cup lettuce leaves, shredded
1/2 cup pomegranate seeds

Directions

Place the flank steak, soy sauce, wine, salt, and black pepper in a ceramic bowl. Let it marinate for 2 hours in your refrigerator. Transfer the meat to a lightly greased cooking basket. Top with parsnips. Add the paprika, onion powder, garlic powder, coriander, and allspice. Cook in the preheated Air Fryer at 400 degrees F for 7 minutes; turn over and cook an additional 5 minutes. In the meantime, make the dressing by mixing olive oil with lime juice and honey. Put the lettuce leaves and roasted parsnip in a salad bowl; toss with the dressing. Slice the steaks and place on top of the salad. Sprinkle over the pomegranate seeds and serve. Enjoy!

Beef and Broccoli Stir-Fry

(Ready in about 20 minutes | Servings 2)

500 Calories; 23.1g Fat; 9.2g Carbs; 65g Protein; 2.4g Sugars

Ingredients

1/2 pound beef stew meat, cut into bite-sized cubes
1/2 pound broccoli, cut into florets
1 small shallot, sliced
1 teaspoon peanut oil
1/2 teaspoon garlic powder
Salt and red pepper, to taste
1 teaspoon Five-spice powder
1 tablespoon fish sauce
1 tablespoon tamari sauce
1 teaspoon sesame seed oil
1 teaspoon Chiu Chow chili sauce

Directions

Toss all ingredients until the beef and veggies are well coated.
Cook in the preheated Air Fryer at 400 degrees F for 6 minutes; shake the basket and continue to air fry for 6 minutes more.
Now, test the meat for doneness, remove the vegetables and cook the meat for 5 minutes more if needed.
Taste and adjust seasonings. Serve immediately.

Argentinian Beef Empanadas

(Ready in about 20 minutes | Servings 2)

630 Calories; 27.3g Fat; 72g Carbs; 22g Protein; 9.7g Sugars

Ingredients

1/2 pound ground chuck
1/2 yellow onion
1 teaspoon fresh garlic, minced
2 tablespoons piri piri sauce
1 tablespoon mustard
6 cubes Cotija cheese
6 Goya discos pastry dough

Directions

Heat a nonstick skillet over medium-high heat. Once hot, cook the ground beef, onion and garlic until tender, about 6 minutes. Crumble with a fork and stir in the piri piri sauce; stir to combine.

Divide the sauce between empanadas. Top with mustard and cheese. Fold each of them in half and seal the edges.

Bake in the preheated Air Fryer at 340 degrees F for about 8 minutes, flipping them halfway through the cooking time. Serve with salsa sauce if desired.

Beef Steak with Zucchini

(Ready in about 20 minutes | Servings 4)

396 Calories; 20.4g Fat; 3.5g Carbs; 47.8g Protein; 0.1g Sugars

Ingredients

1 ½ pounds beef steak
1 pound zucchini
1 teaspoon dried rosemary
1 teaspoon dried basil
1 teaspoon dried oregano
2 tablespoons extra-virgin olive oil
2 tablespoons fresh chives, chopped

Directions

Start by preheating your Air Fryer to 400 degrees F.
Toss the steak and zucchini with the spices and olive oil. Transfer to the cooking basket and cook for 6 minutes.
Now, shale the basket and cook another 6 minutes. Serve immediately garnished with fresh chives. Enjoy!

Best Pretzel

(Ready in about 40 minutes | Servings 4)

553 Calories; 22.1g Fat; 51.1g Carbs; 37.5g Protein; 8.1g Sugars

Ingredients

3/4 pound ground beef
1 smoked beef sausage, chopped
4 scallions, chopped
1 garlic clove, minced
2 tablespoons fresh coriander, chopped
4 tablespoons rolled oats
2 tablespoons tomato paste
Himalayan salt and ground black pepper, to taste
8 small pretzel rolls
4 tablespoons mayonnaise
8 thin slices of tomato

Directions

Start by preheating your Air Fryer to 370 degrees F.
In a mixing bowl, thoroughly combine the ground beef, sausage, scallions, garlic, coriander, oats, tomato paste, salt, and black pepper. Knead with your hands until everything is well combined.
Form the mixture into eight patties and cook them for 18 to 20 minutes. Work in batches.
Place the burgers on slider buns; top with mayonnaise and tomato slices. Bon appétit!

Taco Stuffed Avocados

(Ready in about 15 minutes | Servings 3)

521 Calories; 42.1g Fat; 23.1g Carbs; 20.2g Protein; 4.8g Sugars

Ingredients

1/3 pound ground beef
1 tablespoons shallots, minced
1/2 teaspoon garlic, minced
1 tomato, chopped
1/3 teaspoon Mexican oregano
Salt and black pepper, to taste
1 chipotle pepper in adobo sauce, minced
1/4 cup cilantro
3 avocados, cut into halves and pitted
1/2 cup Cotija cheese, grated

Directions

Preheat a nonstick skillet over medium-high heat. Cook the ground beef and shallot for about 4 minutes.
Stir in the garlic and tomato and continue to sauté for a minute or so. Add in the Mexican oregano, salt, black pepper, chipotle pepper and cilantro.
Then, remove a bit of the pulp from each avocado half and fill them with the taco mixture.
Cook in the preheated Air Fryer at 400 degrees F for 5 minutes. Top with Cotija cheese and continue to cook for 4 minutes more or until cheese is bubbly. Enjoy!

Pastrami and Cheddar Quiche

(Ready in about 20 minutes | Servings 2)

435 Calories; 31.4g Fat; 6.7g Carbs; 30.4g Protein; 3.8g Sugars

Ingredients

4 eggs
1 bell pepper, chopped
2 spring onions, chopped
1 cup pastrami, sliced
1/4 cup Greek-style yogurt
1/2 cup Cheddar cheese, grated
Sea salt, to taste
1/4 teaspoon ground black pepper

Directions

Start by preheating your Air Fryer to 330 degrees F. Spritz the baking pan with cooking oil.

Then, thoroughly combine all ingredients and pour the mixture into the prepared baking pan.

Cook for 7 to 9 minutes or until the eggs have set. Place on a cooling rack and let it sit for 10 minutes before slicing and serving.

Meat Tart

(Ready in about 20 minutes | Servings 3)

496 Calories; 23.3g Fat; 41.2g Carbs; 32.3g Protein; 7g Sugars

Ingredients

6 ounces refrigerated pie crusts
3/4 pound lean ground beef
1/2 onion
1 clove garlic, finely chopped
Sea salt and ground black pepper, to taste
1/2 cup tomato paste
3 Swiss cheese slices
1 egg white, beaten

Directions

Start by preheating your Air Fryer to 360 degrees F.

Cook the ground beef, onion and garlic in a nonstick skillet until the beef is no longer pink and the onion is translucent. Season with salt and pepper; fold in the tomato paste and stir to combine.

Unroll the pie crust and use a round cookie cutter to make 3 even rounds.

Fill the pie crust rounds with the beef mixture. Top with cheese.

Moisten the outside of each round with beaten egg white.

Fold the pie crust rounds in half and use a fork to gently press the edges. Cook at 360 degrees F for about 15 minutes. Serve immediately.

New York Strip with Mustard Butter

(Ready in about 20 minutes | Servings 4)

459 Calories; 27.4g Fat; 2.5g Carbs; 48.3g Protein; 1.4g Sugars

Ingredients

1 tablespoon peanut oil
2 pounds New York Strip
1 teaspoon cayenne pepper
Sea salt and freshly cracked black pepper, to taste
1/2 stick butter, softened
1 teaspoon whole-grain mustard
1/2 teaspoon honey

Directions

Rub the peanut oil all over the steak; season with cayenne pepper, salt, and black pepper.
Cook in the preheated Air Fryer at 400 degrees F for 7 minutes; turn over and cook an additional 7 minutes.
Meanwhile, prepare the mustard butter by whisking the butter, whole-grain mustard, and honey.
Serve the roasted New York Strip dolloped with the mustard butter. Bon appétit!

Mom's Toad in the Hole

(Ready in about 45 minutes | Servings 4)

584 Calories; 40.2g Fat; 29.5g Carbs; 23.4g Protein; 3.4g Sugars

Ingredients

6 beef sausages
1 tablespoon butter, melted
1 cup plain flour
A pinch of salt
2 eggs
1 cup semi-skimmed milk

Directions

Cook the sausages in the preheated Air Fryer at 380 degrees F for 15 minutes, shaking halfway through the cooking time.
Meanwhile, make up the batter mix.
Tip the flour into a bowl with salt; make a well in the middle and crack the eggs into it. Mix with an electric whisk; now, slowly and gradually pour in the milk, whisking all the time.
Place the sausages in a lightly greased baking pan. Pour the prepared batter over the sausages.
Cook in the preheated Air Fryer at 370 degrees F approximately 25 minutes, until golden and risen. Serve with gravy if desired. Bon appétit!

Paprika Porterhouse Steak with Cauliflower

(Ready in about 20 minutes | Servings 4)

196 Calories; 7.8g Fat; 7.5g Carbs; 25.4g Protein; 2.8g Sugars

Ingredients

1 pound Porterhouse steak, sliced
1 teaspoon butter, room temperature
Coarse sea salt and ground black pepper, to taste
1/2 teaspoon shallot powder
1/2 teaspoon porcini powder
1 teaspoon granulated garlic
1 teaspoon smoked paprika
1 pound cauliflower, torn into florets

Directions

Brush the steak with butter on all sides; season it with all spices.
Season the cauliflower with salt and pepper to taste.
Place the steak in the cooking basket and roast at 400 degrees F for 12 minutes; turn over halfway through the cooking time.
Remove the cauliflower from the basket and continue to cook your steak for 2 to 3 minutes if needed.
Serve the steak garnished with the cauliflower. Eat warm.

Beef and Vegetable Stir Fry

(Ready in about 35 minutes + marinating time | Servings 4)

418 Calories; 12.2g Fat; 4.8g Carbs; 68.2g Protein; 2.3g Sugars

Ingredients

1 pounds top round, cut into bite-sized strips
2 garlic cloves, sliced
1 teaspoon dried marjoram
1/4 cup red wine
1 tablespoon tamari sauce
Salt and black pepper, to taste
1 tablespoon olive oil
1 red onion, sliced
2 bell peppers, sliced
1 carrot, sliced

Directions

Place the top round, garlic, marjoram, red wine, tamari sauce, salt and pepper in a bowl, cover and let it marinate for 1 hour.
Preheat your Air Fryer to 390 degrees F and add the oil.
Once hot, discard the marinade and cook the beef for 15 minutes.
Add the onion, peppers, carrot, and garlic and continue cooking until tender about 15 minutes more.
Open the Air Fryer every 5 minutes and baste the meat with the remaining marinade. Serve immediately.

Cuban Mojo Beef

(Ready in about 15 minutes | Servings 3)

263 Calories; 17.4g Fat; 4.1g Carbs; 23.5g Protein; 2g Sugars

Ingredients

3/4 pound blade steak, cut into cubes
1 teaspoon olive oil
Salt and red pepper flakes, to season
Mojo sauce:
1 teaspoon garlic, smashed
2 tablespoons extra-virgin olive oil
2 tablespoons fresh parsley, chopped
2 tablespoons fresh cilantro, chopped
1/2 lime, freshly squeezed
1 green chili pepper, minced

Directions

Toss the steak with olive oil, salt and red pepper.
Cook in your Air Fryer at 400 degrees F for 12 minutes, turning them over halfway through the cooking time.
Meanwhile, make the sauce by mixing all ingredients in your food processor or blender. Serve the warm blade steak with the Mojo sauce on the side. Enjoy!

Classic Beef Ribs

(Ready in about 35 minutes | Servings 4)

532 Calories; 39g Fat; 0.4g Carbs; 44.7g Protein; 0g Sugars

Ingredients

2 pounds beef back ribs
1 tablespoon sunflower oil
1/2 teaspoon mixed peppercorns, cracked
1 teaspoon red pepper flakes
1 teaspoon dry mustard
Coarse sea salt, to taste

Directions

Trim the excess fat from the beef ribs. Mix the sunflower oil, cracked peppercorns, red pepper, dry mustard, and salt.
Rub over the ribs.
Cook in the preheated Air Fryer at 395 degrees F for 11 minutes
Turn the heat to 330 degrees F and continue to cook for 18 minutes more. Serve warm.

Italian Sausage Peperonata Pomodoro

(Ready in about 15 minutes | Servings 2)

473 Calories; 34.6g Fat; 19.3g Carbs; 22.1g Protein; 9.7g Sugars

Ingredients

2 bell peppers, sliced
1 chili pepper
1 yellow onion, sliced
2 smoked beef sausages
1 teaspoon olive oil
2 medium-sized tomatoes, peeled and crushed
1 garlic clove, minced
1 teaspoon Italian spice mix

Directions

Spritz the sides and bottom of the cooking basket with a nonstick cooking oil. Add the peppers, onion and sausage to the cooking basket.

Cook at 390 degrees F for 10 minutes, shaking the basket periodically. Reserve.

Heat the olive oil in a medium-sized saucepan over medium-high flame until sizzling; add in the tomatoes and garlic; let it cook for 2 to 3 minutes.

Stir in the peppers, onion and Italian spice mix. Continue to cook for 1 minute longer or until heated through. Fold in the sausages and serve warm. Bon appétit!

Minty Tender Filet Mignon

(Ready in about 20 minutes + marinating time | Servings 4)

389 Calories; 20.4g Fat; 4.6g Carbs; 47.3g Protein; 1.7g Sugars

Ingredients

2 tablespoons olive oil
2 tablespoons Worcestershire sauce
1 lemon, juiced
1/4 cup fresh mint leaves, chopped
4 cloves garlic, minced
Sea salt and ground black pepper, to taste
2 pounds filet mignon

Directions

In a ceramic bowl, place the olive oil, Worcestershire sauce, lemon juice, mint leaves, garlic, salt, black pepper, and cayenne pepper. Add the fillet mignon and let it marinate for 2 hours in the refrigerator.

Roast in the preheated Air Fryer at 400 degrees F for 18 minutes, basting with the reserved marinade and flipping a couple of times. Serve warm. Bon appétit!

Meatballs with Cranberry Sauce

(Ready in about 40 minutes | Servings 4)

520 Calories; 22.4g Fat; 44g Carbs; 45.4g Protein; 25.5g Sugars

Ingredients

Meatballs:
1 ½ pounds ground chuck
1 egg
1 cup rolled oats
1/2 cup Romano cheese, grated
1/2 teaspoon dried basil
1/2 teaspoon dried oregano
3 teaspoon paprika
4 garlic cloves, minced
2 tablespoons scallions, chopped
Sea salt and cracked black pepper, to taste
Cranberry Sauce:
10 ounces BBQ sauce
8 ounces cranberry sauce

Directions

In a large bowl, mix all ingredients for the meatballs. Mix until everything is well incorporated; then, shape the meat mixture into 2-inch balls using a cookie scoop. Transfer them to the lightly greased cooking basket and cook at 380 degrees F for 10 minutes. Shake the basket occasionally and work in batches. Add the BBQ sauce and cranberry sauce to a saucepan and cook over moderate heat until you achieve a glaze-like consistency; it will take about 15 minutes. Gently stir in the air fried meatballs and cook an additional 3 minutes or until heated through. Enjoy!

Fish

Squid Mediterranean

(Ready in about 10 minutes | Servings 2)

529 Calories; 24.3g Fat; 41g Carbs; 33.2g Protein; 3.2g Sugars

Ingredients

1/2 pound calamari tubes cut into rings, cleaned
Sea salt and ground black pepper, to season
1/2 cup almond flour
1/2 cup all-purpose flour
4 tablespoons parmesan cheese, grated
1/2 cup ale beer
1/4 teaspoon cayenne pepper
1/2 cup breadcrumbs
1/4 cup mayonnaise
1/4 cup Greek-style yogurt
1 clove garlic, minced
1 tablespoon fresh lemon juice
1 teaspoon fresh parsley, chopped
1 teaspoon fresh dill, chopped

Directions

Sprinkle the calamari with salt and black pepper.
Mix the flour, cheese and beer in a bowl until well combined. In another bowl, mix cayenne pepper and breadcrumbs
Dip the calamari pieces in the flour mixture, then roll them onto the breadcrumb mixture, pressing to coat on all sides; transfer them to a lightly oiled cooking basket.
Cook at 400 degrees F for 4 minutes, shaking the basket halfway through the cooking time.
Meanwhile, mix the remaining ingredients until everything is well incorporated. Serve warm calamari with the sauce for dipping.
Enjoy!

Fried Oysters with Lime Sauce

(Ready in about 10 minutes | Servings 2)

295 Calories; 8.7g Fat; 23.4g Carbs; 30g Protein; 3.3g Sugars

Ingredients

8 fresh oysters, shucked
1/3 cup plain flour
1 egg
3/4 cup breadcrumbs
1/2 teaspoon Italian seasoning mix
1 lime, freshly squeezed
1 teaspoon coconut sugar
1 kaffir lime leaf, shredded
1 habanero pepper, minced
1 teaspoon olive oil

Directions

Clean the oysters and set them aside.

Add the flour to a rimmed plate. Whisk the egg in another rimmed plate. Mix the breadcrumbs and Italian seasoning mix in a third plate. Dip your oysters in the flour, shaking off the excess. Then, dip them in the egg mixture and finally, coat your oysters with the breadcrumb mixture.

Spritz the breaded oysters with a nonstick cooking spray.

Cook your oysters in the preheated Air Fryer at 400 degrees F for 2 to 3 minutes, shaking the basket halfway through the cooking time.

Meanwhile, blend the remaining ingredients to make the sauce. Serve the warm oysters with the kaffir lime sauce on the side. Bon appétit!

Cod Frittata

(Ready in about 20 minutes | Servings 3)

454 Calories; 30.8g Fat; 10.3g Carbs; 32.4g Protein; 4.1g Sugars

Ingredients

2 cod fillets
6 eggs
1/2 cup milk
1 shallot, chopped
2 garlic cloves, minced
Sea salt and ground black pepper, to taste
1/2 teaspoon red pepper flakes, crushed

Directions

Bring a pot of salted water to a boil. Boil the cod fillets for 5 minutes or until it is opaque. Flake the fish into bite-sized pieces.
In a mixing bowl, whisk the eggs and milk. Stir in the shallots, garlic, salt, black pepper, and red pepper flakes. Stir in the reserved fish.
Pour the mixture into the lightly greased baking pan.
Cook in the preheated Air Fryer at 360 degrees F for 9 minutes, flipping over halfway through. Bon appétit!

Greek Sardeles

(Ready in about 40 minutes | Servings 2)

349 Calories; 17.5g Fat; 19g Carbs; 26.3g Protein; 4.3g Sugars

Ingredients

4 sardines, cleaned
1/4 cup all-purpose flour
Sea salt and ground black pepper, to taste
4 tablespoons extra-virgin olive oil
1/2 red onion, chopped
1/2 teaspoon fresh garlic, minced
1/4 cup sweet white wine
1 tablespoon fresh coriander, minced
1/4 cup baby capers, drained
1 tomato, crushed
1/4 teaspoon chili paper flakes

Directions

Coat your sardines with all-purpose flour until well coated on all sides.

Season your sardines with salt and black pepper and arrange them in the cooking basket. Cook in your Air Fryer at 325 degrees F for 35 to 40 minutes until the skin is crispy.

Meanwhile, heat olive oil in a frying pan over a moderate flame. Now, sauté the onion and garlic for 4 to 5 minutes or until tender and aromatic.

Stir in the remaining ingredients, cover and let it simmer, for about 15 minutes or until the sauce has thickened and reduced. Spoon the sauce over the warm sardines and serve immediately. Enjoy!

Crispy Tilapia Fillets

(Ready in about 20 minutes | Servings 5)

315 Calories; 9.1g Fat; 19.4g Carbs; 38.5g Protein; 0.7g Sugars

Ingredients

5 tablespoons all-purpose flour
Sea salt and white pepper, to taste
1 teaspoon garlic paste
2 tablespoons extra virgin olive oil
1/2 cup cornmeal
5 tilapia fillets, slice into halves

Directions

Combine the flour, salt, white pepper, garlic paste, olive oil, and cornmeal in a Ziploc bag. Add the fish fillets and shake to coat well. Spritz the Air Fryer basket with cooking spray. Cook in the preheated Air Fryer at 400 degrees F for 10 minutes; turn them over and cook for 6 minutes more. Work in batches.
Serve with lemon wedges if desired. Enjoy!

Baked Sardines with Tangy Dipping Sauce

(Ready in about 45 minutes | Servings 3)

413 Calories; 29.1g Fat; 4g Carbs; 32g Protein; 1.7g Sugars

Ingredients

1 pound fresh sardines
Sea salt and ground black pepper, to taste
1 teaspoon Italian seasoning mix
2 cloves garlic, minced
3 tablespoons olive oil
1/2 lemon, freshly squeezed

Directions

Toss your sardines with salt, black pepper and Italian seasoning mix. Cook in your Air Fryer at 325 degrees F for 35 to 40 minutes until skin is crispy.
Meanwhile, make the sauce by whisking the remaining ingredients
Serve warm sardines with the sauce on the side. Bon appétit!

Glazed Salmon Steaks

(Ready in about 20 minutes | Servings 2)

421 Calories; 16.8g Fat; 19.9g Carbs; 46.7g Protein; 18.1g Sugars

Ingredients

1 salmon steaks
Coarse sea salt, to taste
1/4 teaspoon freshly ground black pepper, or more to taste
2 tablespoons honey
1 tablespoon sesame oil
Zest of 1 lemon
1 tablespoon fresh lemon juice
1 teaspoon garlic, minced
1/2 teaspoon smoked cayenne pepper
1/2 teaspoon dried dill

Directions

Preheat your Air Fryer to 380 degrees F. Pat dry the salmon steaks with a kitchen towel.

In a ceramic dish, combine the remaining ingredients until everything is well whisked.

Add the salmon steaks to the ceramic dish and let them sit in the refrigerator for 1 hour. Now, place the salmon steaks in the cooking basket. Reserve the marinade.

Cook for 12 minutes, flipping halfway through the cooking time.

Meanwhile, cook the marinade in a small sauté pan over a moderate flame. Cook until the sauce has thickened.

Pour the sauce over the steaks and serve with mashed potatoes if desired. Bon appétit!

Marinated Flounder Filets

(Ready in about 15 minutes + marinating time | Servings 3)

376 Calories; 14g Fat; 24.5g Carbs; 34.1g Protein; 4.8g Sugars

Ingredients

1 pound flounder filets
1 teaspoon garlic, minced
2 tablespoons soy sauce
1 teaspoon Dijon mustard
1/4 cup malt vinegar
1 teaspoon granulated sugar
Salt and black pepper, to taste
1/2 cup plain flour
1 egg
2 tablespoons milk
1/2 cup parmesan cheese, grated

Directions

Place the flounder filets, garlic, soy sauce, mustard, vinegar and sugar in a glass bowl; cover and let it marinate in your refrigerator for at least 1 hour. Transfer the fish to a plate, discarding the marinade. Salt and pepper to taste. Place the plain flour in a shallow bowl; in another bowl, beat the egg and milk until pale and well combined; add parmesan cheese to the third bowl. Dip the flounder filets in the flour, then in the egg mixture; repeat the process and coat them with the parmesan cheese, pressing to adhere.

Cook the flounder filets in the preheated Air Fryer at 400 degrees F for 5 minutes; turn the flounder filets over and cook on the other side for 5 minutes more. Enjoy!

Tuna Steaks with Pearl Onions

(Ready in about 20 minutes | Servings 4)

332 Calories; 5.9g Fat; 10.5g Carbs; 56.1g Protein; 6.1g Sugars

Ingredients

4 tuna steaks
1 pound pearl onions
4 teaspoons olive oil
1 teaspoon dried rosemary
1 teaspoon dried marjoram
1 tablespoon cayenne pepper
1/2 teaspoon sea salt
1/2 teaspoon black pepper, preferably freshly cracked
1 lemon, sliced

Directions

Place the tuna steaks in the lightly greased cooking basket. Top with the pearl onions; add the olive oil, rosemary, marjoram, cayenne pepper, salt, and black pepper.

Bake in the preheated Air Fryer at 400 degrees F for 9 to 10 minutes. Work in two batches.

Serve warm with lemon slices and enjoy!

Monkfish with Sautéed Vegetables and Olives

(Ready in about 20 minutes | Servings 2)

310 Calories; 13.3g Fat; 12.7g Carbs; 35.2g Protein; 5.4g Sugars

Ingredients

2 teaspoons olive oil
2 carrots, sliced
2 bell peppers, sliced
1 teaspoon dried thyme
1/2 teaspoon dried marjoram
1/2 teaspoon dried rosemary
2 monkfish fillets
1 tablespoon soy sauce
2 tablespoons lime juice
Coarse salt and ground black pepper, to taste
1 teaspoon cayenne pepper
1/2 cup Kalamata olives, pitted and sliced

Directions

In a nonstick skillet, heat the olive oil for 1 minute. Once hot, sauté the carrots and peppers until tender, about 4 minutes. Sprinkle with thyme, marjoram, and rosemary and set aside.

Toss the fish fillets with the soy sauce, lime juice, salt, black pepper, and cayenne pepper. Place the fish fillets in a lightly greased cooking basket and bake at 390 degrees F for 8 minutes.

Turn them over, add the olives, and cook an additional 4 minutes. Serve with the sautéed vegetables on the side. Bon appétit!

Swordfish with Cherry Tomatoes

(Ready in about 15 minutes | Servings 3)

291 Calories; 13.5g Fat; 10.4g Carbs; 31.9g Protein; 6.8g Sugars

Ingredients

1 pound swordfish steak
1/2 cup cornflakes, crushed
1 teaspoon Old Bay seasoning
Salt and black pepper, to season
2 teaspoon olive oil
1 pound cherry tomatoes

Directions

Toss the swordfish steak with cornflakes, Old Bay seasoning, salt, black pepper and 1 teaspoon of olive oil.

Cook the swordfish steak in your Air Fryer at 400 degrees F for 6 minutes.

Now, turn the fish over, top with tomatoes and drizzle with the remaining teaspoon of olive oil. Continue to cook for 4 minutes.

Serve with lemon slices if desired. Bon appétit!

Masala Fish

(Ready in about 25 minutes | Servings 2)

301 Calories; 12.1g Fat; 2.3g Carbs; 43g Protein; 1.6g Sugars

Ingredients

2 teaspoons olive oil
1/4 cup coconut milk
1/2 teaspoon cayenne pepper
1 teaspoon Garam masala
1/4 teaspoon Kala namak (Indian black salt)
1/2 teaspoon fresh ginger, grated
1 garlic clove, minced
2 catfish fillets
1/4 cup coriander, roughly chopped

Directions

Preheat your Air Fryer to 390 degrees F. Then, spritz the baking dish with a nonstick cooking spray.
In a mixing bowl, whisk the olive oil, milk, cayenne pepper, Garam masala, Kala namak, ginger, and garlic.
Coat the catfish fillets with the Garam masala mixture. Cook the catfish fillets in the preheated Air Fryer approximately 18 minutes, turning over halfway through the cooking time.
Garnish with fresh coriander and serve over hot noodles if desired.

Pollack Fillets with Sticky Sauce

(Ready in about 20 minutes | Servings 2)

573 Calories; 38.3g Fat; 31.5g Carbs; 26.2g Protein; 5.7g Sugars

Ingredients

2 pollack fillets
Salt and black pepper, to taste
1 tablespoon olive oil
1 cup chicken broth
2 tablespoons light soy sauce
1 tablespoon brown sugar
2 tablespoons butter, melted
1 teaspoon fresh ginger, minced
1 teaspoon fresh garlic, minced
2 corn tortillas

Directions

Pat dry the pollack fillets and season them with salt and black pepper; drizzle the sesame oil all over the fish fillets.
Preheat the Air Fryer to 380 degrees F and cook your fish for 11 minutes. Slice into bite-sized pieces.
Meanwhile, prepare the sauce. Add the broth to a large saucepan and bring to a boil. Add the soy sauce, sugar, butter, ginger, and garlic. Reduce the heat to simmer and cook until it is reduced slightly.
Add the fish pieces to the warm sauce. Serve on corn tortillas and enjoy!

Salmon and Fennel Salad

(Ready in about 20 minutes | Servings 3)

306 Calories; 16.3g Fat; 5.6g Carbs; 32.2g Protein; 3g Sugars

Ingredients

1 pound salmon
1 fennel, quartered
1 teaspoon olive oil
Sea salt and ground black pepper, to taste
1/2 teaspoon paprika
1 tablespoon balsamic vinegar
1 tablespoon lime juice
1 tablespoon extra-virgin olive oil
1 tomato, sliced
1 cucumber, sliced
1 tablespoon sesame seeds, lightly toasted

Directions

Toss the salmon and fennel with 1 teaspoon of olive oil, salt, black pepper and paprika.

Cook in the preheated Air Fryer at 380 degrees F for 12 minutes; shaking the basket once or twice.

Cut the salmon into bite-sized strips and transfer them to a nice salad bowl. Add in the fennel, balsamic vinegar, lime juice, 1 tablespoon of extra-virgin olive oil, tomato and cucumber.

Toss to combine well and serve garnished with lightly toasted sesame seeds. Enjoy!

Filet of Flounder Cutlets

(Ready in about 15 minutes | Servings 2)

330 Calories; 20.3g Fat; 12.1g Carbs; 24.8g Protein; 2.3g Sugars

Ingredients

1 egg
1/2 cup cracker crumbs
1/2 cup Pecorino Romano cheese, grated
Sea salt and white pepper, to taste
1/2 teaspoon cayenne pepper
1 teaspoon dried parsley flakes
2 flounder fillets

Directions

To make a breading station, whisk the egg until frothy.
In another bowl, mix the cracker crumbs, Pecorino Romano cheese, and spices.
Dip the fish in the egg mixture and turn to coat evenly; then, dredge in the cracker crumb mixture, turning a couple of times to coat evenly.
Cook in the preheated Air Fryer at 390 degrees F for 5 minutes; turn them over and cook another 5 minutes. Enjoy!

Easiest Lobster Tails Ever

(Ready in about 10 minutes | Servings 2)

147 Calories; 3.5g Fat; 2.5g Carbs; 25.5g Protein; 1.1g Sugars

Ingredients

2 (6-ounce) lobster tails
1 teaspoon fresh cilantro, minced
1/2 teaspoon dried rosemary
1/2 teaspoon garlic, pressed
1 teaspoon deli mustard
Sea salt and ground black pepper, to taste
1 teaspoon olive oil

Directions

Toss the lobster tails with the other ingredients until they are well coated on all sides.

Cook the lobster tails at 370 degrees F for 3 minutes. Then, turn them and cook on the other side for 3 to 4 minutes more until they are opaque.

Serve warm and enjoy!

Monkfish Fillets with Romano Cheese

(Ready in about 15 minutes | Servings 2)

415 Calories; 22.5g Fat; 3.7g Carbs; 47.4g Protein; 2.3g Sugars

Ingredients

1 monkfish fillets
1 teaspoon garlic paste
2 tablespoons butter, melted
1/2 teaspoon Aleppo chili powder
1/2 teaspoon dried rosemary
1/4 teaspoon cracked black pepper
1/2 teaspoon sea salt
4 tablespoons Romano cheese, grated

Directions

Start by preheating the Air Fryer to 320 degrees F. Spritz the Air Fryer basket with cooking oil.
Spread the garlic paste all over the fish fillets.
Brush the monkfish fillets with the melted butter on both sides.
Sprinkle with the chili powder, rosemary, black pepper, and salt.
Cook for 7 minutes in the preheated Air Fryer.
Top with the Romano cheese and continue to cook for 2 minutes more or until heated through. Bon appétit!

Halibut with Thai Lemongrass Marinade

(Ready in about 45 minutes | Servings 2)

359 Calories; 16.7g Fat; 7.8g Carbs; 43.4g Protein; 2.9g Sugars

Ingredients

1 tablespoons tamari sauce
2 tablespoons fresh lime juice
2 tablespoons olive oil
1 teaspoon Thai curry paste
1/2 inch lemongrass, finely chopped
1 teaspoon basil
2 cloves garlic, minced
2 tablespoons shallot, minced
Sea salt and ground black pepper, to taste
2 halibut steaks

Directions

Place all ingredients in a ceramic dish; let it marinate for 30 minutes.
Place the halibut steaks in the lightly greased cooking basket.
Bake in the preheated Air Fryer at 400 degrees F for 9 to 10 minutes, basting with the reserved marinade and flipping them halfway through the cooking time. Bon appétit!

Homemade Fish Fingers

(Ready in about 15 minutes | Servings 2)

332 Calories; 10.5g Fat; 12.2g Carbs; 46.3g Protein; 2.8g Sugars

Ingredients

3/4 pound tilapia
1 egg
2 tablespoons milk
4 tablespoons chickpea flour
1/4 cup pork rinds
1/2 cup breadcrumbs
1/2 teaspoon red chili flakes
Coarse sea salt and black pepper, to season

Directions

Rinse the tilapia and pat it dry using kitchen towels. Then, cut the tilapia into strips.
Then, whisk the egg, milk and chickpea flour in a rimmed plate.
Add the pork rinds and breadcrumbs to another plate; stir in red chili flakes, salt and black pepper and stir to combine well.
Dip the fish strips in the egg mixture, then, roll them over the breadcrumb mixture. Transfer the fish fingers to the Air Fryer cooking basket and spritz them with a nonstick cooking spray.
Cook in the preheated Air Fryer at 400 degrees F for 10 minutes, shaking the basket halfway through to ensure even browning. Serve warm and enjoy!

Indian Famous Fish Curry

(Ready in about 25 minutes | Servings 4)

449 Calories; 29.1g Fat; 20.4g Carbs; 27.3g Protein; 13.3g Sugars

Ingredients

1 tablespoons sunflower oil
1/2 pound fish, chopped
2 red chilies, chopped
1 tablespoon coriander powder
1 teaspoon curry paste
1 cup coconut milk
Salt and white pepper, to taste
1/2 teaspoon fenugreek seeds
1 shallot, minced
1 garlic clove, minced
1 ripe tomato, pureed

Directions

Preheat your Air Fryer to 380 degrees F; brush the cooking basket with 1 tablespoon of sunflower oil.

Cook your fish for 10 minutes on both sides. Transfer to the baking pan that is previously greased with the remaining tablespoon of sunflower oil.

Add the remaining ingredients and reduce the heat to 350 degrees F. Continue to cook an additional 10 to 12 minutes or until everything is heated through. Enjoy!

Salmon with Baby Bok Choy

(Ready in about 20 minutes | Servings 3)

308 Calories; 13.6g Fat; 12.2g Carbs; 34.3g Protein; 9.3g Sugars

Ingredients

1 pound salmon filets
1 teaspoon garlic chili paste
1 teaspoon sesame oil
1 tablespoon honey
1 tablespoon soy sauce
1 pound baby Bok choy, bottoms removed
Kosher salt and black pepper, to taste

Directions

Start by preheating your Air Fryer to 380 degrees F.

Toss the salmon fillets with garlic chili paste, sesame oil, honey, soy sauce, salt and black pepper.

Cook the salmon in the preheated Air Fryer for 6 minutes; turn the filets over and cook an additional 6 minutes.

Then, cook the baby Bok choy at 350 degrees F for 3 minutes; shake the basket and cook an additional 3 minutes. Salt and pepper to taste.

Serve the salmon fillets with the roasted baby Bok choy. Enjoy!

Mediterranean Calamari Salad

(Ready in about 15 minutes | Servings 3)

457 Calories; 31.3g Fat; 18.4g Carbs; 25.1g Protein; 9.2g Sugars

Ingredients

1 pound squid, cleaned, sliced into rings
2 tablespoons sherry wine
1/2 teaspoon granulated garlic
Salt, to taste
1/2 teaspoon ground black pepper
1/2 teaspoon basil
1/2 teaspoon dried rosemary
1 cup grape tomatoes
1 small red onion, thinly sliced
1/3 cup Kalamata olives, pitted and sliced
1/2 cup mayonnaise
1 teaspoon yellow mustard
1/2 cup fresh flat-leaf parsley leaves, coarsely chopped

Directions

Start by preheating the Air Fryer to 400 degrees F. Spritz the Air Fryer basket with cooking oil.

Toss the squid rings with the sherry wine, garlic, salt, pepper, basil, and rosemary. Cook in the preheated Air Fryer for 5 minutes, shaking the basket halfway through the cooking time.

Work in batches and let it cool to room temperature. When the squid is cool enough, add the remaining ingredients.

Gently stir to combine and serve well chilled. Bon appétit!

Shrimp Kabobs with Cherry Tomatoes

(Ready in about 30 minutes | Servings 4)

267 Calories; 6.8g Fat; 18.1g Carbs; 35.4g Protein; 14.5g Sugars

Ingredients

1 ½ pounds jumbo shrimp, cleaned, shelled and deveined
1 pound cherry tomatoes
2 tablespoons butter, melted
1 tablespoons Sriracha sauce
Sea salt and ground black pepper, to taste
1/2 teaspoon dried oregano
1/2 teaspoon dried basil
1 teaspoon dried parsley flakes
1/2 teaspoon marjoram
1/2 teaspoon mustard seeds

Directions

Toss all ingredients in a mixing bowl until the shrimp and tomatoes are covered on all sides.
Soak the wooden skewers in water for 15 minutes.
Thread the jumbo shrimp and cherry tomatoes onto skewers. Cook in the preheated Air Fryer at 400 degrees F for 5 minutes, working with batches. Bon appétit!

Anchovy and Cheese Wontons

(Ready in about 15 minutes | Servings 2)

473 Calories; 25.1g Fat; 19.4g Carbs; 41g Protein; 4.9g Sugars

Ingredients

1/2 pound anchovies
1/2 cup cheddar cheese, grated
1 cup fresh spinach
2 tablespoons scallions, minced
1 teaspoon garlic, minced
1 tablespoon Shoyu sauce
Himalayan salt and ground black pepper, to taste
1/2 pound wonton wrappers
1 teaspoon sesame oil

Directions

Mash the anchovies and mix with the cheese, spinach, scallions, garlic and Shoyu sauce; season with salt and black pepper and mix to combine well.
Fill your wontons with 1 tablespoon of the filling mixture and fold into triangle shape; brush the side with a bit of oil and water to seal the edges.
Cook in your Air Fryer at 390 degrees F for 10 minutes, flipping the wontons for even cooking. Enj

Sea Bass with French Sauce Tartare

(Ready in about 15 minutes | Servings 2)

384 Calories; 28.5g Fat; 3.5g Carbs; 27.6g Protein; 1g Sugars

Ingredients

1 tablespoon olive oil
2 sea bass fillets
Sauce:
1/2 cup mayonnaise
1 tablespoon capers, drained and chopped
1 tablespoon gherkins, drained and chopped
2 tablespoons scallions, finely chopped
2 tablespoons lemon juice

Directions

Start by preheating your Air Fryer to 395 degrees F. Drizzle olive oil all over the fish fillets.

Cook the sea bass in the preheated Air Fryer for 10 minutes, flipping them halfway through the cooking time.

Meanwhile, make the sauce by whisking the remaining ingredients until everything is well incorporated. Place in the refrigerator until ready to serve. Bon appétit!

Vegetable and Side Dishes

Sweet Baby Carrots

(Ready in about 45 minutes | Servings 3)

157 Calories; 4.8g Fat; 29.3g Carbs; 1.2g Protein; 22.4g Sugars

Ingredients

1 tablespoon coconut oil
1 pound baby carrots
1 teaspoon fresh ginger, peeled and grated
2 lemongrasses, finely chopped
3 tablespoons honey
1 teaspoon lemon thyme

Directions

Toss all ingredients in a mixing bowl and let it stand for 30 minutes.
Transfer the baby carrots to the cooking basket.
Cook the baby carrots at 380 degrees F for 15 minutes, shaking the basket halfway through the cooking time to ensure even cooking.
Serve warm and enjoy!

Fried Green Beans with Pecorino Romano

(Ready in about 15 minutes | Servings 3)

340 Calories; 9.7g Fat; 50.9g Carbs; 12.8g Protein; 4.7g Sugars

Ingredients

1 tablespoons buttermilk
1 egg
4 tablespoons cornmeal
4 tablespoons tortilla chips, crushed
4 tablespoons Pecorino Romano cheese, finely grated
Coarse salt and crushed black pepper, to taste
1 teaspoon smoked paprika
12 ounces green beans, trimmed

Directions

In a shallow bowl, whisk together the buttermilk and egg.
In a separate bowl, combine the cornmeal, tortilla chips, Pecorino Romano cheese, salt, black pepper, and paprika.
Dip the green beans in the egg mixture, then, in the cornmeal/cheese mixture. Place the green beans in the lightly greased cooking basket.
Cook in the preheated Air Fryer at 390 degrees F for 4 minutes. Shake the basket and cook for a further 3 minutes.
Taste, adjust the seasonings, and serve with the dipping sauce if desired. Bon appétit!

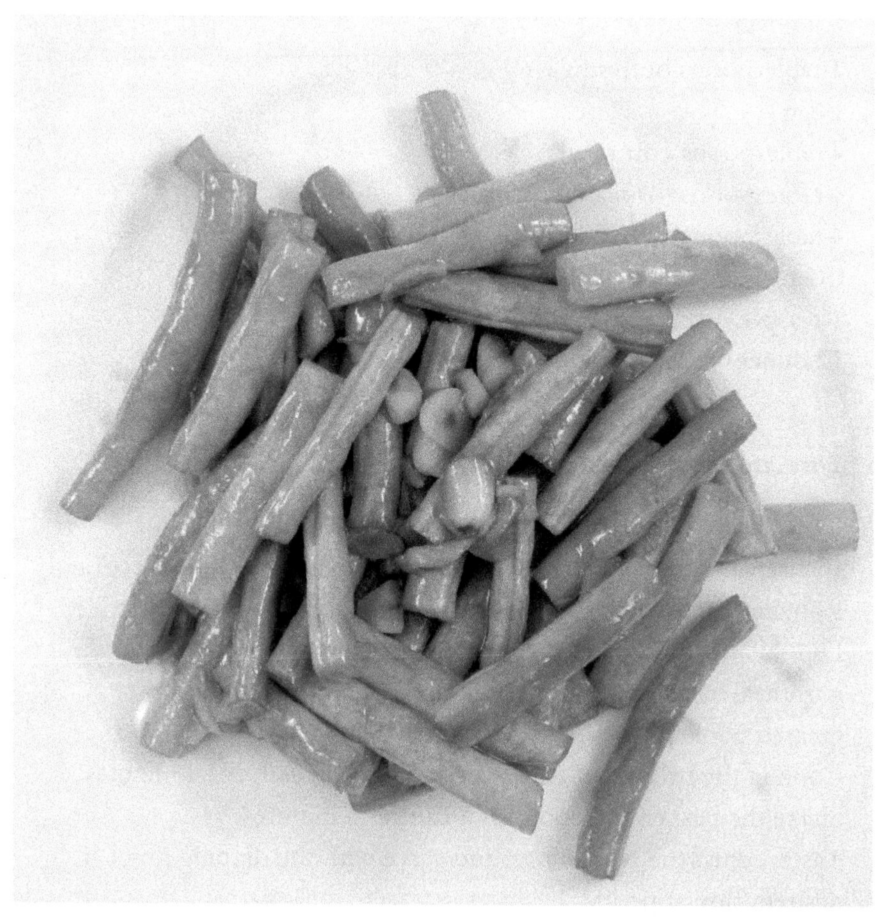

Mexican-Style Avocado

(Ready in about 10 minutes | Servings 4)

267 Calories; 16.7g Fat; 27g Carbs; 5.9g Protein; 1.9g Sugars

Ingredients

2 ripe avocados, peeled and cut wedges
1/2 cup plain flour
Himalayan salt and ground white pepper, to taste
1 egg
2 tablespoons milk
1/2 cup tortilla chips, crushed

Directions

Start by preheating your Air Fryer to 395 degrees F.
In a shallow bowl, combine the flour, salt and black pepper. In another shallow dish, whisk the egg and milk until frothy.
Place the crushed tortilla chips in a third shallow dish. Dip the avocado wedges in the flour mixture, shaking off the excess. Then, dip in the egg mixture; lastly, coat the avocado wedges with crushed tortilla chips, pressing to adhere.
Spritz the avocado wedges with cooking oil on all sides.
Cook your avocado in the preheated Air Fryer at 395 degrees F for approximately 8 minutes, turning them over halfway through the cooking time. Bon appétit!

Roasted Broccoli with Sesame

(Ready in about 15 minutes | Servings 2)

267 Calories; 19.5g Fat; 20.2g Carbs; 8.9g Protein; 5.2g Sugars

Ingredients

1 pound broccoli florets
2 tablespoons sesame oil
1/2 teaspoon shallot powder
1/2 teaspoon porcini powder
1 teaspoon garlic powder
Sea salt and ground black pepper, to taste
1/2 teaspoon cumin powder
1/4 teaspoon paprika
2 tablespoons sesame seeds

Directions

Start by preheating the Air Fryer to 400 degrees F.
Blanch the broccoli in salted boiling water until al dente, about 3 to 4 minutes. Drain well and transfer to the lightly greased Air Fryer basket.
Add the sesame oil, shallot powder, porcini powder, garlic powder, salt, black pepper, cumin powder, paprika, and sesame seeds.
Cook for 6 minutes, tossing halfway through the cooking time. Bon appétit!

Brussels Sprouts with Bacon

(Ready in about 20 minutes | Servings 2)

277 Calories; 19.2g Fat; 18.7g Carbs; 11.6g Protein; 5.4g Sugars

Ingredients

3/4 pound Brussels sprouts, trimmed and halved
1 teaspoon butter, melted
Sea salt and ground black pepper, to taste
1/2 teaspoon smoked paprika
1 teaspoon garlic, minced
1 teaspoon lemon juice, freshly squeezed
1 tablespoon white wine
3 ounces bacon, sliced

Directions

Toss the Brussels sprouts with butter, salt, black pepper, paprika, garlic, lemon juice and wine. Transfer your Brussels sprouts to the Air Fryer cooking basket.

Top your Brussels sprouts with bacon and cook them at 380 degrees F for 15 minutes, shaking the basket once or twice to ensure even cooking.

Serve warm and enjoy!

Double-Cheese Stuffed Mushrooms

(Ready in about 20 minutes | Servings 2)

267 Calories; 19.6g Fat; 7.2g Carbs; 17.3g Protein; 2.9g Sugars

Ingredients

8 medium-sized button mushrooms, stalks removed
1 teaspoon butter
1 teaspoon garlic, minced
Sea salt and ground black pepper, to taste
4 ounces Ricotta cheese, at room temperature
1/2 cup Romano cheese, grated
1/2 teaspoon ancho chili powder

Directions

Clean your mushrooms and place them on a platter.
Then, mix the remaining ingredients in a bowl. Divide the filling between your mushrooms and transfer them to a lightly greased cooking basket.
Cook the mushrooms in the preheated Air Fryer at 380 degrees for 10 to 12 minutes. Serve warm and enjoy!

Spicy Roasted Potatoes

(Ready in about 15 minutes | Servings 2)

299 Calories; 13.6g Fat; 40.9g Carbs; 4.8g Protein; 1.4g Sugars

Ingredients

4 potatoes, peeled and cut into wedges
2 tablespoons olive oil
Sea salt and ground black pepper, to taste
1 teaspoon cayenne pepper
1/2 teaspoon ancho chili powder

Directions

Toss all ingredients in a mixing bowl until the potatoes are well covered.
Transfer them to the Air Fryer basket and cook at 400 degrees F for 6 minutes; shake the basket and cook for a further 6 minutes.
Serve warm with your favorite sauce for dipping. Bon appétit!

Baked Cauliflower

(Ready in about 20 minutes | Servings 4)

153 Calories; 7.3g Fat; 19.3g Carbs; 4.1g Protein; 2.9g Sugars

Ingredients

1/2 cup all-purpose flour
1/2 cup water
Salt, to taste
1/2 teaspoon ground black pepper
1/2 teaspoon shallot powder
1/2 teaspoon garlic powder
1/2 teaspoon cayenne pepper
1 tablespoons olive oil
1 pound cauliflower, broken into small florets
1/4 cup Cholula sauce

Directions

Start by preheating your Air Fryer to 400 degrees F. Lightly grease a baking pan with cooking spray.

In a mixing bowl, combine the flour, water, spices, and olive oil.

Coat the cauliflower with the prepared batter; arrange the cauliflower on the baking pan.

Then, bake in the preheated Air Fryer for 8 minutes or until golden brown.

Brush the Cholula sauce all over the cauliflower florets and bake an additional 4 to 5 minutes. Bon appétit!

Mediterranean Vegetable Skewers

(Ready in about 30 minutes | Servings 4)

138 Calories; 10.2g Fat; 10.2g Carbs; 2.2g Protein; 6.6g Sugars

Ingredients

1 medium-sized zucchini, cut into 1-inch pieces
2 red bell peppers, cut into 1-inch pieces
1 green bell pepper, cut into 1-inch pieces
1 red onion, cut into 1-inch pieces
2 tablespoons olive oil
Sea salt, to taste
1/2 teaspoon black pepper, preferably freshly cracked
1/2 teaspoon red pepper flakes

Directions

Soak the wooden skewers in water for 15 minutes.
Thread the vegetables on skewers; drizzle olive oil all over the vegetable skewers; sprinkle with spices.
Cook in the preheated Air Fryer at 400 degrees F for 13 minutes.
Serve warm and enjoy!

Mediterranean-Style Roasted Broccoli

(Ready in about 10 minutes | Servings 3)

199 Calories; 15.6g Fat; 11.3g Carbs; 4.6g Protein; 2.8g Sugars

Ingredients

1 pound broccoli florets
1 teaspoon butter, melted
Sea salt, to taste
1 teaspoon mixed peppercorns, crushed
1/4 cup mayonnaise
1 tablespoon fresh lemon juice
1 teaspoon deli mustard
2 cloves garlic, minced

Directions

Toss the broccoli florets with butter, salt and crushed peppercorns until well coated on all sides.

Cook in the preheated Air Fryer at 400 degrees F for 6 minutes until they've softened.

In the meantime, make your aioli by mixing the mayo, lemon juice, mustard and garlic in a bowl.

Serve the roasted broccoli with the sauce on the side. Enjoy!

Crispy Button Mushrooms

(Ready in about 10 minutes | Servings 3)

157 Calories; 1.3g Fat; 28.2g Carbs; 10.4g Protein; 3.2g Sugars

Ingredients

1/2 cup flour
1 tablespoons milk
2 eggs
1 cup fresh breadcrumbs
1/2 teaspoon garlic powder
1/4 teaspoon mustard seeds
1/4 teaspoon cumin powder
1/4 teaspoon ground bay leaf
1/2 teaspoon onion powder
1/2 teaspoon cayenne pepper
Kosher salt and ground pepper, to taste
1 pound button mushrooms, cleaned and cut into half

Directions

Place the flour in a shallow bowl. Then, in another shallow bowl, beat the milk and eggs until pale and frothy.

Then, in a third bowl, thoroughly combine the breadcrumbs with all spices.

Dip the mushrooms into the flour until coated on all sides. Then dip the mushrooms into the egg mixture. Lastly, roll your mushrooms onto the spiced breadcrumb mixture until well coated.

Place the mushrooms in your Air Fryer and spritz them with a nonstick cooking spray. Cook the mushrooms at 380 degrees F for 6 minutes, shaking the basket halfway through the cooking time.

Serve warm with your favorite dipping sauce. Bon appétit!

Swiss Cheese & Vegetable Casserole

(Ready in about 50 minutes | Servings 4)

328 Calories; 16.5g Fat; 33.1g Carbs; 13.1g Protein; 7.6g Sugars

Ingredients

1 pound potatoes, peeled and sliced (1/4-inch thick)
2 tablespoons olive oil
1/2 teaspoon red pepper flakes, crushed
1/2 teaspoon freshly ground black pepper
Salt, to taste
3 bell peppers, thinly sliced
1 serrano pepper, thinly sliced
2 medium-sized tomatoes, sliced
1 leek, thinly sliced
2 garlic cloves, minced
1 cup Swiss cheese, shredded

Directions

Start by preheating your Air Fryer to 350 degrees F. Spritz a casserole dish with cooking oil. Place the potatoes in the casserole dish in an even layer; drizzle 1 tablespoon of olive oil over the top. Then, add the red pepper, black pepper, and salt. Add 2 bell peppers and 1/2 of the leeks. Add the tomatoes and the remaining 1 tablespoon of olive oil. Add the remaining peppers, leeks, and minced garlic. Top with the cheese.

Cover the casserole with foil and bake for 32 minutes. Remove the foil and increase the temperature to 400 degrees F; bake an additional 16 minutes. Bon appétit!

Twice-Baked Potatoes with Pancetta

(Ready in about 30 minutes | Servings 5)

401 Calories; 7.7g Fat; 69.9g Carbs; 15.2g Protein; 3.8g Sugars

Ingredients

2 teaspoons canola oil
5 large russet potatoes, peeled
Sea salt and ground black pepper, to taste
5 slices pancetta, chopped
5 tablespoons Swiss cheese, shredded

Directions

Start by preheating your Air Fryer to 360 degrees F.
Drizzle the canola oil all over the potatoes. Place the potatoes in the Air Fryer basket and cook approximately 20 minutes, shaking the basket periodically.
Lightly crush the potatoes to split and season them with salt and ground black pepper. Add the pancetta and cheese.
Place in the preheated Air Fryer and bake an additional 5 minutes or until cheese has melted. Bon appétit!

Greek-Style Air Grilled Tomatoes with Feta

(Ready in about 15 minutes | Servings 3)

147 Calories; 11.2g Fat; 7.6g Carbs; 5.2g Protein; 5.1g Sugars

Ingredients

3 medium tomatoes, quartered, pat dry
1 tablespoon extra-virgin olive oil
1 teaspoon basil
1 teaspoon oregano
1/2 teaspoon rosemary
1 teaspoon parsley
1 teaspoon cilantro
Sea salt and ground black pepper, to season
2 tablespoons Greek black olives, pitted and sliced
3 ounces feta cheese, sliced

Directions

Brush your tomatoes with olive oil. Sprinkle them with spices until well coated on all sides. Now, transfer your tomatoes to the Air Fryer cooking basket

Cook your tomatoes at 350 degrees F for approximately 12 minutes, turning them over halfway through the cooking time.

Garnish with black olives and feta cheese and serve. Enjoy!

Crispy Parmesan Asparagus

(Ready in about 20 minutes | Servings 4)

207 Calories; 12.4g Fat; 11.7g Carbs; 12.2g Protein; 1.6g Sugars

Ingredients

2 eggs
1 teaspoon Dijon mustard
1 cup Parmesan cheese, grated
1 cup bread crumbs
Sea salt and ground black pepper, to taste
18 asparagus spears, trimmed
1/2 cup sour cream

Directions

Start by preheating your Air Fryer to 400 degrees F.

In a shallow bowl, whisk the eggs and mustard. In another shallow bowl, combine the Parmesan cheese, breadcrumbs, salt, and black pepper.

Dip the asparagus spears in the egg mixture, then in the parmesan mixture; press to adhere.

Cook for 5 minutes; work in three batches. Serve with sour cream on the side. Enjoy!

Sweet Potato Hash Browns

(Ready in about 50 minutes | Servings 3)

188 Calories; 6.2g Fat; 30.4g Carbs; 4g Protein; 3.1g Sugars

Ingredients

1 pound sweet potatoes, grated
1/2 cup scallion, chopped
1 bell pepper, chopped
1/2 teaspoon garlic, finely chopped
Sea salt and ground black pepper, to your liking
1 teaspoon peanut oil
1/4 teaspoon ground allspice
1 tablespoon peanut oil

Directions

Allow your sweet potatoes to soak for 25 minutes in cold water. Drain the water and pat them dry with a paper towel.
Add in the remaining ingredients and stir until everything is well combined.
Cook in the preheated Air Fryer at 395 degrees F for 25 minutes, turning them over halfway through the cooking time. Bon appétit!

Greek-Style Vegetable Bake

(Ready in about 35 minutes | Servings 4)

296 Calories; 22.9g Fat; 16.1g Carbs; 9.3g Protein; 9.9g Sugars

Ingredients

1 eggplant, peeled and sliced
2 bell peppers, seeded and sliced
1 red onion, sliced
1 teaspoon fresh garlic, minced
4 tablespoons olive oil
1 teaspoon mustard
1 teaspoon dried oregano
1 teaspoon smoked paprika
Salt and ground black pepper, to taste
1 tomato, sliced
6 ounces halloumi cheese, sliced lengthways

Directions

Start by preheating your Air Fryer to 370 degrees F. Spritz a baking pan with nonstick cooking spray.
Place the eggplant, peppers, onion, and garlic on the bottom of the baking pan. Add the olive oil, mustard, and spices. Transfer to the cooking basket and cook for 14 minutes.
Top with the tomatoes and cheese; increase the temperature to 390 degrees F and cook for 5 minutes more until bubbling. Let it sit on a cooling rack for 10 minutes before serving.
Bon appétit!

Charred Asparagus and Cherry Tomato Salad

(Ready in about 10 minutes + chilling time | Servings 4)

289 Calories; 16.7g Fat; 30.1g Carbs; 8.9g Protein; 19.9g Sugars

Ingredients

1/4 cup olive oil
1 pound asparagus, trimmed
1 pound cherry tomatoes
1/4 cup balsamic vinegar
2 garlic cloves, minced
2 scallion stalks, chopped
1/2 teaspoon oregano
Coarse sea salt and ground black pepper, to your liking
2 hard-boiled eggs, sliced

Directions

Start by preheating your Air Fryer to 400 degrees F. Brush the cooking basket with 1 tablespoon of olive oil.

Add the asparagus and cherry tomatoes to the cooking basket. Drizzle 1 tablespoon of olive oil all over your veggies.

Cook for 5 minutes, shaking the basket halfway through the cooking time. Let it cool slightly.

Toss with the remaining olive oil, balsamic vinegar, garlic, scallions, oregano, salt, and black pepper.

Afterwards, add the hard-boiled eggs on the top of your salad and serve.

Rainbow Vegetable Fritters

(Ready in about 20 minutes | Servings 2)

215 Calories; 8.4g Fat; 31.6g Carbs; 6g Protein; 4.1g Sugars

Ingredients

1 zucchini, grated and squeezed
1 cup corn kernels
1/2 cup canned green peas
4 tablespoons all-purpose flour
2 tablespoons fresh shallots, minced
1 teaspoon fresh garlic, minced
1 tablespoon peanut oil
Sea salt and ground black pepper, to taste
2 teaspoon cayenne pepper

Directions

In a mixing bowl, thoroughly combine all ingredients until everything is well incorporated.
Shape the mixture into patties. Spritz the Air Fryer basket with cooking spray.
Cook in the preheated Air Fryer at 365 degrees F for 6 minutes.
Turn them over and cook for a further 6 minutes
Serve immediately and enjoy!

Fried Peppers with Roasted Garlic Sauce

(Ready in about 50 minutes | Servings 2)

307 Calories; 26.2g Fat; 16.3g Carbs; 4.2g Protein; 6.1g Sugars

Ingredients

4 bell peppers
1 teaspoon olive oil
Sea salt and black pepper to taste
1 tablespoon fresh parsley, roughly chopped
Dipping Sauce:
6 cloves garlic
1/4 cup sour cream
1/4 cup mayonnaise
1 teaspoon fresh lime juice
1/4 teaspoon paprika

Directions

Brush the peppers with olive oil and transfer them to the cooking basket. Roast the peppers at 400 degrees F for 15 minutes, turning your peppers over halfway through the cooking time; roast the peppers until the skin blisters and turns black.

Transfer the peppers to a plastic bag until cool; the skins should peel away off of the peppers easily; season the peppers with salt and pepper and reserve.

To make the sauce, place the garlic on a sheet of aluminum foil and spritz with cooking spray. Wrap the garlic in the foil.

Cook in the preheated Air Fryer at 400 degrees for 12 minutes. Then, open the top of the foil and continue to cook for a further 10 minutes.

Let it cool for about 10 minutes; remove the cloves by squeezing them out of the skins; mash the garlic and combine it with the sour cream, mayonnaise, fresh lime juice and paprika.

Garnish the roasted peppers with parsley and serve with the sauce on the side and enjoy!

Classic Roasted Potatoes with Scallion Dip

(Ready in about 15 minutes | Servings 2)

567 Calories; 27g Fat; 72g Carbs; 11.3g Protein; 8.1g Sugars

Ingredients

4 medium-sized potatoes, peeled and cut into wedges
1 tablespoon olive oil
1/2 teaspoon ancho chili powder
1/2 teaspoon dried marjoram
1/2 teaspoon dried basil
Sea salt and ground black pepper, to taste
1/2 cup cream cheese
3 tablespoons scallions, sliced

Directions

Toss the potatoes with olive oil and spices until well coated.
Transfer them to the Air Fryer basket and cook at 400 degrees F for 6 minutes; shake the basket and cook for a further 6 minutes.
Meanwhile, whisk the cheese with the scallions and place the sauce in your refrigerator until ready to use.
Serve the warm potatoes with the sauce for dipping. Bon appétit!

Greek-Style Roasted Tomatoes with Feta

(Ready in about 20 minutes | Servings 2)

148 Calories; 9.4g Fat; 9.4g Carbs; 7.8g Protein; 6.6g Sugars

Ingredients

3 medium-sized tomatoes, cut into four slices, pat dry
1 teaspoon dried basil
1 teaspoon dried oregano
1/4 teaspoon red pepper flakes, crushed
1/2 teaspoon sea salt
3 slices Feta cheese

Directions

Spritz the tomatoes with cooking oil and transfer them to the Air Fryer basket. Sprinkle with seasonings.
Cook at 350 degrees F approximately 8 minutes turning them over halfway through the cooking time.
Top with the cheese and cook an additional 4 minutes. Bon appétit!

Roasted Broccoli and Cauliflower with Tahini Sauce

(Ready in about 15 minutes | Servings 3)

178 Calories; 11.9g Fat; 14.6g Carbs; 6.8g Protein; 4.8g Sugars

Ingredients

1/2 pound broccoli, broken into florets
1/2 pound cauliflower, broken into florets
1 teaspoon onion powder
1/2 teaspoon porcini powder
1/4 teaspoon cumin powder
1/2 teaspoon granulated garlic
1 teaspoon olive oil
3 tablespoons tahini
2 tablespoons soy sauce
1 teaspoon white vinegar
Salt and chili flakes, to taste

Directions

Start by preheating your Air Fryer to 400 degrees F.
Now, toss the vegetables with the onion powder, porcini powder cumin powder, garlic and olive oil. Transfer your vegetables to the lightly greased cooking basket.
Air Fry your veggies in the preheated Air Fryer at 400 degrees F for 6 minutes. Remove the broccoli florets from the cooking basket.
Continue to cook the cauliflower for 5 to 6 minutes more.
Meanwhile, make the tahini sauce by simply whisking the remaining ingredients in a small bowl.
Spoon the sauce over the warm vegetables and serve immediately.
Bon appétit!

Spicy Ricotta Stuffed Mushrooms

(Ready in about 35 minutes | Servings 4)

214 Calories; 5.6g Fat; 30.4g Carbs; 12.3g Protein; 5g Sugars

Ingredients

1/2 pound small white mushrooms
Sea salt and ground black pepper, to taste
1 tablespoons Ricotta cheese
1/2 teaspoon ancho chili powder
1 teaspoon paprika
4 tablespoons all-purpose flour
2 egg
1/2 cup fresh breadcrumbs

Directions

Remove the stems from the mushroom caps and chop them; mix the chopped mushrooms steams with the salt, black pepper, cheese, chili powder, and paprika.
Stuff the mushroom caps with the cheese filling.
Place the flour in a shallow bowl, and beat the egg in another bowl. Place the breadcrumbs in a third shallow bowl.
Dip the mushrooms in the flour, then, dip in the egg mixture; finally, dredge in the breadcrumbs and press to adhere. Spritz the stuffed mushrooms with cooking spray.
Cook in the preheated Air Fryer at 360 degrees F for 18 minutes.
Bon appétit!

Italian Peperonata Classica

(Ready in about 25 minutes | Servings 4)

389 Calories; 18.4g Fat; 49.1g Carbs; 9.3g Protein; 19.8g Sugars

Ingredients

1 tablespoons olive oil
4 bell peppers, seeded and sliced
1 serrano pepper, seeded and sliced
1/2 cup onion, peeled and sliced
2 garlic cloves, crushed
2 tomatoes, pureed
2 tablespoons tomato ketchup
Sea salt and black pepper
1 teaspoon cayenne pepper
4 fresh basil leaves
10 Sicilian olives green, pitted and sliced
2 Ciabatta rolls

Directions

Brush the sides and bottom of the cooking basket with 1 tablespoon of olive oil. Add the peppers, onions, and garlic to the cooking basket. Cook for 5 minutes or until tender.

Add the tomatoes, ketchup, salt, black pepper, and cayenne pepper; add the remaining tablespoon of olive oil and cook in the preheated Air Fryer at 380 degrees F for 15 minutes, stirring occasionally.

Divide between individual bowls and garnish with basil leaves and olives. Serve with the Ciabatta rolls. Bon appétit!

SNACKS & APPETIZERS

Sea Scallops and Bacon

(Ready in about 10 minutes | Servings 2)

403 Calories; 22g Fat; 4.3g Carbs; 43.6g Protein; 0g Sugars

Ingredients

10 sea scallops, frozen
4 ounces bacon, diced
1 teaspoon garlic powder
1 teaspoon paprika
Sea salt and ground black pepper, to taste

Directions

Assemble the skewers alternating sea scallops and bacon. Sprinkle the garlic powder, paprika, salt and black pepper all over your kabobs.

Bake your kabobs in the preheated Air Fryer at 400 degrees F for 6 minutes.

Serve warm with your favorite sauce for dipping. Enjoy!

Barbecue Little Smokies

(Ready in about 20 minutes | Servings 6)

182 Calories; 4.6g Fat; 19.2g Carbs; 15.9g Protein; 15.7g Sugars

Ingredients

1 pound beef cocktail wieners
10 ounces barbecue sauce

Directions

Start by preheating your Air Fryer to 380 degrees F.
Prick holes into your sausages using a fork and transfer them to the baking pan.
Cook for 13 minutes. Spoon the barbecue sauce into the pan and cook an additional 2 minutes.
Serve with toothpicks. Bon appétit!

Parsnip Chips with Spicy Citrus

(Ready in about 20 minutes | Servings 4)

207 Calories; 12.1g Fat; 23.8g Carbs; 2.8g Protein; 7g Sugars

Ingredients

1 pound parsnips, peel long strips
2 tablespoons sesame oil
Sea salt and ground black pepper, to taste
1 teaspoon red pepper flakes, crushed
1/2 teaspoon curry powder
1/2 teaspoon mustard seeds
Spicy Citrus Aioli:
1/4 cup mayonnaise
1 tablespoon fresh lime juice
1 clove garlic, smashed
Salt and black pepper, to taste

Directions

Start by preheating the Air Fryer to 380 degrees F.
Toss the parsnip chips with the sesame oil, salt, black pepper, red pepper, curry powder, and mustard seeds.
Cook for 15 minutes, shaking the Air Fryer basket periodically.
Meanwhile, make the sauce by whisking the mayonnaise, lime juice, garlic, salt, and pepper.
Place in the refrigerator until ready to use. Bon appétit!

Pork Crackling with Sriracha Dip

(Ready in about 40 minutes | Servings 3)

525 Calories; 49.8g Fat; 10.6g Carbs; 6.8g Protein; 5.6g Sugars

Ingredients

1/2 pound pork rind
Sea salt and ground black pepper, to taste
1/2 cup tomato sauce
1 teaspoon Sriracha sauce
1/2 teaspoon stone-ground mustard

Directions

Rub sea salt and pepper on the skin side of the pork rind. Allow it to sit for 30 minutes.
Then, cut the pork rind into chunks using kitchen scissors.
Roast the pork rind at 380 degrees F for 8 minutes; turn them over and cook for a further 8 minutes or until blistered.
Meanwhile, mix the tomato sauce with the Sriracha sauce and mustard. Serve the pork crackling with the Sriracha dip and enjoy!

Puerto Rican Tostones

(Ready in about 15 minutes | Servings 2)

151 Calories; 7.1g Fat; 23.9g Carbs; 0.6g Protein; 10.7g Sugars

Ingredients

1 ripe plantain, sliced
1 tablespoon sunflower oil
A pinch of grated nutmeg
A pinch of kosher salt

Directions

Toss the plantains with the oil, nutmeg, and salt in a bowl.
Cook in the preheated Air Fryer at 400 degrees F for 10 minutes, shaking the cooking basket halfway through the cooking time.
Adjust the seasonings to taste and serve immediately

Parmesan Squash Chips

(Ready in about 20 minutes | Servings 3)

174 Calories; 6.1g Fat; 26.1g Carbs; 6.4g Protein; 9.3g Sugars

Ingredients

3/4 pound butternut squash, cut into thin rounds
1/2 cup Parmesan cheese, grated
Sea salt and ground black pepper, to taste
1 teaspoon butter
1/2 cup ketchup
1 teaspoon Sriracha sauce

Directions

Toss the butternut squash with Parmesan cheese, salt, black pepper and butter.
Transfer the butternut squash rounds to the Air Fryer cooking basket.
Air Fryer at 400 degrees F for 12 minutes. Shake the Air Fryer basket periodically to ensure even cooking. Work with batches.
While the parmesan squash chips are baking, whisk the ketchup and sriracha and set it aside.
Serve the parmesan squash chips with Sriracha ketchup and enjoy!

Chili-Lime French Fries

(Ready in about 20 minutes | Servings 3)

128 Calories; 1.9g Fat; 26.6g Carbs; 2.8g Protein; 2.2g Sugars

Ingredients

1 pound potatoes, peeled and cut into matchsticks
1 teaspoon olive oil
1 lime, freshly squeezed
1 teaspoon chili powder
Sea salt and ground black pepper, to taste

Directions

Toss your potatoes with the remaining ingredients until well coated.
Transfer your potatoes to the Air Fryer cooking basket.
Cook the French fries at 370 degrees F for 9 minutes. Shake the cooking basket and continue to cook for about 9 minutes. Serve immediately. Bon appétit!

Meatball Skewers

(Ready in about 20 minutes | Servings 6)

218 Calories; 13g Fat; 10.7g Carbs; 14.1g Protein; 8.5g Sugars

Ingredients

1/2 pound ground pork
1/2 pound ground beef
1 teaspoon dried onion flakes
1 teaspoon fresh garlic, minced
1 teaspoon dried parsley flakes
Salt and black pepper, to taste
1 red pepper, 1-inch pieces
1 cup pearl onions
1/2 cup barbecue sauce

Directions

Mix the ground meat with the onion flakes, garlic, parsley flakes, salt, and black pepper. Shape the mixture into 1-inch balls.
Thread the meatballs, pearl onions, and peppers alternately onto skewers.
Microwave the barbecue sauce for 10 seconds.
Cook in the preheated Air Fryer at 380 degrees for 5 minutes. Turn the skewers over halfway through the cooking time. Brush with the sauce and cook for a further 5 minutes. Work in batches.
Serve with the remaining barbecue sauce and enjoy!

Asian Chicken Wings

(Ready in about 20 minutes | Servings 6)

195 Calories; 5.7g Fat; 9.4g Carbs; 25.5g Protein; 6.4g Sugars

Ingredients

1 ½ pounds chicken wings
2 teaspoons sesame oil
Kosher salt and ground black pepper, to taste
2 tablespoons tamari sauce
1 tablespoon rice vinegar
2 garlic clove, minced
2 tablespoons honey
2 sun-dried tomatoes, minced

Directions

Toss the chicken wings with the sesame oil, salt, and pepper. Add chicken wings to a lightly greased baking pan.
Roast the chicken wings in the preheated Air Fryer at 390 degrees F for 7 minutes. Turn them over once or twice to ensure even cooking.
In a mixing dish, thoroughly combine the tamari sauce, vinegar, garlic, honey, and sun-dried tomatoes.
Pour the sauce all over the chicken wings; bake an additional 5 minutes. Bon appétit!

Sweet Potato Chips with Chili Mayo

(Ready in about 35 minutes | Servings 3)

218 Calories; 19.6g Fat; 9.5g Carbs; 1g Protein; 1.9g Sugars

Ingredients

1 sweet potato, cut into 1/8-inch-thick slices
1 teaspoon olive oil
Sea salt and cracked mixed peppercorns, to taste
1/2 teaspoon turmeric powder
1/3 cup mayonnaise
1 teaspoon granulated garlic
1/2 teaspoon red chili flakes

Directions

Toss the sweet potato slices with olive oil, salt, cracked peppercorns and turmeric powder.

Cook your sweet potatoes at 380 degrees F for 33 to 35 minutes, tossing the basket every 10 minutes to ensure even cooking. Work with batches.

Meanwhile, mix the mayonnaise, garlic and red chili flakes to make the sauce.

The sweet potato chips will crisp up as it cools. Serve the sweet potato chips with the chili mayo on the side.

Mozzarella Sticks

(Ready in about 10 minutes | Servings 3)

270 Calories; 3.7g Fat; 23.1g Carbs; 36.2g Protein; 5.7g Sugars

Ingredients

2 eggs
1/4 cup corn flour
1/4 cup plain flour
1 cup Italian-style dried breadcrumbs
1 teaspoon Italian seasoning mix
10 ounces mozzarella, cut into 1/2-inch sticks
1 cup marinara sauce

Directions

Beat the eggs in a shallow bowl until pale and frothy. Then, in a second bowl, place both types of flour. In a third bowl, mix breadcrumbs with Italian seasoning mix.

Dip the mozzarella sticks in the beaten eggs and allow the excess egg to drip back into the bowl. Then, dip the mozzarella sticks in the flour mixture. Lastly, roll them over the seasoned breadcrumbs.

Cook the mozzarella sticks in the preheated Air Fryer at 370 degrees F for 4 minutes. Flip them over and continue to cook for 2 to 3 minutes more.

Serve the mozzarella sticks with marinara sauce. Bon appétit!

Green Bean Crisps

(Ready in about 20 minutes | Servings 4)

164 Calories; 10.2g Fat; 13.1g Carbs; 6.1g Protein; 1.1g Sugars

Ingredients

1 egg, beaten
1/4 cup cornmeal
1/4 cup parmesan, grated
1 teaspoon sea salt
1/2 teaspoon red pepper flakes, crushed
1 pound green beans
2 tablespoons grapeseed oil

Directions

In a mixing bowl, combine together the egg, cornmeal, parmesan, salt, and red pepper flakes; mix to combine well.
Dip the green beans into the batter and transfer them to the cooking basket. Brush with the grapeseed oil.
Cook in the preheated Air Fryer at 390 degrees F for 4 minutes.
Shake the basket and cook for a further 3 minutes. Work in batches.
Taste, adjust the seasonings and serve. Bon appétit!

Kale Chips with Tahini Sauce

(Ready in about 15 minutes | Servings 4)

170 Calories; 15g Fat; 7.1g Carbs; 4.2g Protein; 0.7g Sugars

Ingredients

4 cups kale leaves, torn into 1-inch pieces
1 ½ tablespoons sesame oil
1/2 teaspoon shallot powder
1 teaspoon garlic powder
1/4 teaspoon porcini powder
1/2 teaspoon mustard seeds
1 teaspoon salt
1/3 cup tahini (sesame butter)
1 tablespoon fresh lemon juice
2 cloves garlic, minced

Directions

Toss the kale with the sesame oil and seasonings.
Bake in the preheated Air Fryer at 350 degrees F for 10 minutes, shaking the cooking basket occasionally.
Bake until the edges are brown. Work in batches.
Meanwhile, make the sauce by whisking all ingredients in a small mixing bowl. Serve and enjoy!

Cocktail Sausage and Veggies on a Stick

(Ready in about 25 minutes | Servings 4)

190 Calories; 6.8g Fat; 18.5g Carbs; 13.3g Protein; 10.3g Sugars

Ingredients

16 cocktail sausages, halved
16 pearl onions
1 red bell pepper, cut into 1 ½-inch pieces
1 green bell pepper, cut into 1 ½-inch pieces
Salt and cracked black pepper, to taste
1/2 cup tomato chili sauce

Directions

Thread the cocktail sausages, pearl onions, and peppers alternately onto skewers. Sprinkle with salt and black pepper.
Cook in the preheated Air Fryer at 380 degrees for 15 minutes, turning the skewers over once or twice to ensure even cooking.
Serve with the tomato chili sauce on the side. Enjoy!

Mustard Brussels Sprout Chips

(Ready in about 25 minutes | Servings 2)

112 Calories; 7.2g Fat; 10.3g Carbs; 3.9g Protein; 2.5g Sugars

Ingredients

1/2 pound Brussels sprouts, cut into small pieces
1 teaspoon deli mustard
1 teaspoon sesame oil
1 teaspoon champagne vinegar
1/4 teaspoon paprika
1/4 teaspoon cayenne pepper
Coarse sea salt and ground black pepper, to taste

Directions

Start by preheating your Air Fryer to 360 degrees F.

Toss the Brussels sprouts with the other ingredients until well coated. Transfer the Brussels sprouts to the Air Fryer cooking basket.

Cook the Brussels sprout chips in the preheated Air Fryer for about 20 minutes, shaking the basket every 6 to 7 minutes.

Serve with your favorite sauce for dipping. Enjoy!

Root Vegetable Chips with Dill Mayonnaise

(Ready in about 40 minutes | Servings 4)

187 Calories; 11.2g Fat; 20.1g Carbs; 2.6g Protein; 11.2g Sugars

Ingredients

1/2 pound red beetroot, julienned
1/2 pound golden beetroot, julienned
1/4 pound carrot, julienned
Sea salt and ground black pepper, to taste
1 teaspoon olive oil
1/2 cup mayonnaise
1 teaspoon garlic, minced
1/4 teaspoon dried dill weed

Directions

Toss your veggies with salt, black pepper and olive oil.
Arrange the veggie chips in a single layer in the Air Fryer cooking basket.
Cook the veggie chips in the preheated Air Fryer at 340 degrees F for 20 minutes; tossing the basket occasionally to ensure even cooking. Work with two batches.
Meanwhile, mix the mayonnaise, garlic and dill until well combined.
Serve the vegetable chips with the mayo sauce on the side. Bon appétit!

Greek-Style Squash Chips

(Ready in about 25 minutes | Servings 4)

180 Calories; 10.3g Fat; 13.3g Carbs; 5.8g Protein; 2.8g Sugars

Ingredients

1/2 cup seasoned breadcrumbs
1/2 cup Parmesan cheese, grated
Sea salt and ground black pepper, to taste
1/4 teaspoon oregano
2 yellow squash, cut into slices
2 tablespoons grapeseed oil Sauce:
1/2 cup Greek-style yogurt
1 tablespoon fresh cilantro, chopped
1 garlic clove, minced
Freshly ground black pepper, to your liking

Directions

In a shallow bowl, thoroughly combine the seasoned breadcrumbs, Parmesan, salt, black pepper, and oregano.

Dip the yellow squash slices in the prepared batter, pressing to adhere.

Brush with the grapeseed oil and cook in the preheated Air Fryer at 400 degrees F for 12 minutes. Shake the Air Fryer basket periodically to ensure even cooking. Work in batches.

While the chips are baking, whisk the sauce ingredients; place in your refrigerator until ready to serve. Enjoy!

Mini Turkey and Corn Burritos

(Ready in about 25 minutes | Servings 6)

242 Calories; 13.6g Fat; 19.9g Carbs; 13.7g Protein; 2.1g Sugars

Ingredients

1 tablespoon olive oil
1/2 pound ground turkey
2 tablespoons shallot, minced
1 garlic clove, smashed
1 red bell pepper, seeded and chopped
1 ancho chili pepper, seeded and minced
1/2 teaspoon ground cumin
Sea salt and freshly ground black pepper, to taste
1/3 cup salsa
6 ounces sweet corn kernels
12 (8-inch) tortilla shells
1 tablespoon butter, melted
1/2 cup sour cream, for serving

Directions

Heat the olive oil in a sauté pan over medium-high heat. Cook the ground meat and shallots for 3 to 4 minutes. Add the garlic and peppers and cook an additional 3 minutes or until fragrant. After that, add the spices, salsa, and corn. Stir until everything is well combined. Place about 2 tablespoons of the meat mixture in the center of each tortilla. Roll your tortillas to seal the edges and make the burritos. Brush each burrito with melted butter and place them in the lightly greased cooking basket. Bake at 395 degrees F for 10 minutes, turning them over halfway through the cooking time. Garnish each burrito with a dollop of sour cream and serve.

Sticky Glazed Wings

(Ready in about 30 minutes | Servings 2)

318 Calories; 19.3g Fat; 11.6g Carbs; 22.1g Protein; 10.2g Sugars

Ingredients

1/2 pound chicken wings
1 tablespoon sesame oil
2 tablespoons brown sugar
1 tablespoon Worcestershire sauce
1 tablespoon hot sauce
1 tablespoon balsamic vinegar

Directions

Brush the chicken wings with sesame oil and transfer them to the Air Fryer cooking basket.

Cook the chicken wings at 370 degrees F for 12 minutes; turn them over and cook for a further 10 minutes.

Meanwhile, bring the other ingredients to a boil in a saucepan; cook for 2 to 3 minutes or until thoroughly cooked.

Toss the warm chicken wings with the sauce and place them on a serving platter. Serve and enjoy!

Crunchy Broccoli Fries

(Ready in about 15 minutes | Servings 4)

127 Calories; 8.6g Fat; 9.9g Carbs; 4.9g Protein; 2.6g Sugars

Ingredients

1 pound broccoli florets
1/2 teaspoon onion powder
1 teaspoon granulated garlic
1/2 teaspoon cayenne pepper
Sea salt and ground black pepper, to taste
2 tablespoons sesame oil
5 tablespoons parmesan cheese, preferably freshly grated

Directions

Start by preheating the Air Fryer to 400 degrees F.
Blanch the broccoli in salted boiling water until al dente, about 3 to 4 minutes. Drain well and transfer to the lightly greased Air Fryer basket.
Add the onion powder, garlic, cayenne pepper, salt, black pepper, and sesame oil.
Cook for 6 minutes, tossing halfway through the cooking time. Bon appétit!

Paprika Potato Chips

(Ready in about 50 minutes | Servings 3)

190 Calories; 0.3g Fat; 43.8g Carbs; 4.7g Protein; 6.1g Sugars

Ingredients

3 potatoes, thinly sliced
1 teaspoon sea salt
1 teaspoon garlic powder
1 teaspoon paprika
1/4 cup ketchup

Directions

Add the sliced potatoes to a bowl with salted water. Let them soak for 30 minutes. Drain and rinse your potatoes.
Pat dry and toss with salt.
Cook in the preheated Air Fryer at 400 degrees F for 15 minutes, shaking the basket occasionally.
Work in batches. Toss with the garlic powder and paprika. Serve with ketchup. Enjoy!

Cauliflower Bombs with Sweet & Sour Sauce

(Ready in about 25 minutes | Servings 4)

156 Calories; 11.9g Fat; 7.2g Carbs; 6.9g Protein; 3.3g Sugars

Ingredients

Cauliflower Bombs:
1/2 pound cauliflower
2 ounces Ricotta cheese
1/3 cup Swiss cheese
1 egg
1 tablespoon Italian seasoning mix
Sweet & Sour Sauce:
1 red bell pepper, jarred
1 clove garlic, minced
1 teaspoon sherry vinegar
1 tablespoon tomato puree
2 tablespoons olive oil
Salt and black pepper, to taste

Directions

Blanch the cauliflower in salted boiling water about 3 to 4 minutes until al dente. Drain well and pulse in a food processor.
Add the remaining ingredients for the cauliflower bombs; mix to combine well.
Bake in the preheated Air Fryer at 375 degrees F for 16 minutes, shaking halfway through the cooking time.
In the meantime, pulse all ingredients for the sauce in your food processor until combined. Season to taste. Serve the cauliflower bombs with the Sweet & Sour Sauce on the side. Bon appétit!

Pork Crackling with Sriracha Dip

(Ready in about 40 minutes | Servings 3)

525 Calories; 49.8g Fat; 10.6g Carbs; 6.8g Protein; 5.6g Sugars

Ingredients

1/2 pound pork rind
Sea salt and ground black pepper, to taste
1/2 cup tomato sauce
1 teaspoon Sriracha sauce
1/2 teaspoon stone-ground mustard

Directions

Rub sea salt and pepper on the skin side of the pork rind. Allow it to sit for 30 minutes.
Then, cut the pork rind into chunks using kitchen scissors.
Roast the pork rind at 380 degrees F for 8 minutes; turn them over and cook for a further 8 minutes or until blistered.
Meanwhile, mix the tomato sauce with the Sriracha sauce and mustard. Serve the pork crackling with the Sriracha dip and enjoy!

Easy and Delicious Pizza Puffs

(Ready in about 15 minutes | Servings 6)

186 Calories; 12g Fat; 12.4g Carbs; 6.5g Protein; 3.6g Sugars

Ingredients

6 ounces crescent roll dough
1/2 cup mozzarella cheese, shredded
3 ounces pepperoni
3 ounces mushrooms, chopped
1 teaspoon oregano
1 teaspoon garlic powder
1/4 cup Marina sauce, for dipping

Directions

Unroll the crescent dough. Roll out the dough using a rolling pin; cut into 6 pieces.
Place the cheese, pepperoni, and mushrooms in the center of each pizza puff. Sprinkle with oregano and garlic powder.
Fold each corner over the filling using wet hands. Press together to cover the filling entirely and seal the edges.
Now, spritz the bottom of the Air Fryer basket with cooking oil. Lay the pizza puffs in a single layer in the cooking basket. Work in batches.
Bake at 370 degrees F for 5 to 6 minutes or until golden brown. Serve with the marinara sauce for dipping.

Mexican Cheesy Zucchini Bites

(Ready in about 25 minutes | Servings 4)

231 Calories; 9g Fat; 29.3g Carbs; 8.4g Protein; 2.3g Sugars

Ingredients

1 large-sized zucchini, thinly sliced
1/2 cup flour
1/4 cup yellow cornmeal
1 egg, whisked
1/2 cup tortilla chips, crushed
1/2 cup Queso Añejo, grated
Salt and cracked pepper, to taste

Directions

Pat dry the zucchini slices with a kitchen towel.
Mix the remaining ingredients in a shallow bowl; mix until everything is well combined. Dip each zucchini slice in the prepared batter.
Cook in the preheated Air Fryer at 400 degrees F for 12 minutes, shaking the basket halfway through the cooking time.
Work in batches until the zucchini slices are crispy and golden brown. Enjoy!

Rice and Grains

Easy Cornbread

(Ready in about 20 minutes | Servings 4)

196 Calories; 12.4g Fat; 18.6g Carbs; 2.5g Protein; 5.8g Sugars

Ingredients

1/2 cup self-rising cornmeal mix
A dash of salt
A dash of grated nutmeg
A dash of granulated sugar
1 tablespoon honey
4 tablespoons butter, melted
1/2 cup full-fat milk

Directions

In a mixing bowl, thoroughly combine the dry ingredients. In another bowl, mix the wet ingredients.
Then, stir the wet mixture into the dry mixture.
Pour the batter into a lightly buttered baking pan. Now, bake your cornbread at 340 degrees F for about 15 minutes.
Check for doneness and transfer to a wire rack to cool slightly before cutting and serving. Bon appétit!

Cheese Risotto Balls

(Ready in about 35 minutes | Servings 3)

505 Calories; 21.4g Fat; 60g Carbs; 13.9g Protein; 4.8g Sugars

Ingredients

1 cup Arborio rice
2 tablespoons butter
2 ounces Provolone cheese, grated
2 ounces Asiago cheese, grated
1 egg, whisked
1/3 cup seasoned breadcrumbs, passed through a sieve
1 tablespoon olive oil
1/4 cup leeks, chopped
9 ounces canned San Marzano tomatoes
1 teaspoon red pepper flakes, crushed
2 tablespoons fresh basil leaves, roughly chopped
Sea salt and freshly cracked black pepper, to taste

Directions

Bring 3 cups of water to a boil in a saucepan over medium-high heat. Stir in the rice and reduce the heat to simmer; cook for about 20 minutes. Fluff your rice in a mixing bowl; stir in the butter and cheese. Salt and pepper to taste; shape the mixture into equal balls. Beat the egg in a shallow bowl; in another shallow bowl, place the seasoned breadcrumbs. Dip each rice ball into the beaten egg, then, roll in the seasoned breadcrumbs, gently pressing to adhere. Bake the rice balls in the preheated Air Fryer at 350 degrees F for about 10 minutes, shaking the basket halfway through the cooking time to ensure even cooking. Meanwhile, heat the olive oil in a saucepan over a moderate flame. Once hot, sauté the leeks until just tender and fragrant. Now, add in the tomatoes and spices and let it simmer for about 25 minutes, breaking your tomatoes with a spatula. Serve the warm risotto balls with Arrabbiata sauce for dipping. Bon appétit!

Polenta Fries with Sriracha Sauce

(Ready in about 45 minutes + chilling time | Servings 3)

247 Calories; 6.5g Fat; 43.8g Carbs; 3.7g Protein; 11.5g Sugars

Ingredients

Polenta Fries:
1 ½ cups water
1 teaspoon sea salt
1/2 cup polenta
1 tablespoon butter, room temperature
A pinch of grated nutmeg
1 teaspoon dried Italian herb mix Sriracha Sauce:
1 red jalapeno pepper, minced
1 garlic clove, minced
1 tablespoon cider vinegar
2 tablespoons tomato paste
1 tablespoon honey

Directions

Bring the water and 1 teaspoon sea salt to a boil in a saucepan; slowly and gradually stir in the polenta, whisking continuously until there are no lumps. Reduce the heat to simmer and cook for 5 to 6 minutes until the polenta starts to thicken. Cover and continue to simmer for 25 minutes or until you have a thick mixture, whisking periodically. Stir in the butter, nutmeg, and Italian herbs. Pour your polenta into a parchment-lined rimmed baking tray, spreading the mixture evenly. Cover with plastic wrap; let it stand in your refrigerator for about 2 hours to firm up. Then, slice the polenta into strips and place them in the greased Air Fryer basket. Cook in the preheated Air Fryer at 395 degrees F for about 11 minutes. Meanwhile, make the Sriracha sauce by whisking all ingredients. Serve the warm polenta fries with the Sriracha sauce on the side. Enjoy!

Classic Rizzi Bizzi

(Ready in about 35 minutes | Servings 2)

444 Calories; 5.7g Fat; 86g Carbs; 12.1g Protein; 6.3g Sugars

Ingredients

1 cup long-grain brown rice, soaked overnight
1 carrot, grated
1 cup green peas, fresh or thawed
1/4 cup Shoyu sauce
1 teaspoon sesame oil

Directions

Add the brown rice and 2 cups of water to a saucepan. Bring to a boil.
Cover and reduce the heat to a slow simmer. Cook your rice for 30 minutes, then, fluff it with a fork.
Combine your rice with the remaining ingredients and transfer it to the cooking basket.
Cook your rizzi bizzi at 340 degrees F for about 13 minutes, stirring halfway through the cooking time. Serve immediately!

Taco Stuffed Bread

(Ready in about 15 minutes | Servings 4)

472 Calories; 21.9g Fat; 37.6g Carbs; 30.5g Protein; 6.6g Sugars

Ingredients

1 loaf French bread
1/2 pound ground beef
1 onion, chopped
1 teaspoon garlic, minced
1 package taco seasoning
1 ½ cups Queso Panela, sliced
Salt and ground black pepper, to taste
3 tablespoons tomato paste
2 tablespoons fresh cilantro leaves, chopped

Directions

Cut the top off of the loaf of bread; remove some of the bread from the middle creating a well and reserve.
In a large skillet, cook the ground beef with the onion and garlic until the beef is no longer pink and the onion is translucent.
Add the taco seasoning, cheese, salt, black pepper, and tomato paste. Place the taco mixture into your bread.
Bake in the preheated Air Fryer at 380 degrees F for 5 minutes.
Garnish with fresh cilantro leaves. Enjoy!

Mexicana Air Grilled Fish Tacos

(Ready in about 15 minutes | Servings 3)

422 Calories; 11.5g Fat; 41.3g Carbs; 39g Protein; 3.3g Sugars

Ingredients

1 pound tilapia filets
1 teaspoon chipotle powder
1 teaspoon fresh coriander, finely chopped
1 teaspoon fresh garlic, minced
1 teaspoon extra-virgin olive oil
1 teaspoon taco seasoning mix
1 cup pickled cabbage, drained and shredded
6 mini taco shells

Directions

Toss the tilapia filets with the chipotle powder, coriander, garlic, olive oil and taco seasoning mix.

Cook the fish in your Air Fryer at 400 degrees F for 10 minutes, flipping halfway through the cooking time.

Remove the tilapia filets to a cutting board then flake into pieces.

To assemble the tacos, divide the fish and pickled cabbage between taco shells. Roll them up and transfer to the Air Fryer cooking basket.

Bake your tacos at 360 degrees F for 5 minutes until thoroughly warmed. Bon appétit!

Mediterranean Monkey Bread

(Ready in about 20 minutes | Servings 6)

427 Calories; 25.4g Fat; 38.1g Carbs; 11.6g Protein; 6.5g Sugars

Ingredients

1 (16-ounce) can refrigerated buttermilk biscuits
3 tablespoons olive oil
1 cup Provolone cheese, grated
1/4 cup black olives, pitted and chopped
4 tablespoons basil pesto
1/4 cup pine nuts, chopped
1 tablespoon Mediterranean herb mix

Directions

Separate your dough into the biscuits and cut each of them in half; roll them into balls. Dip each ball into the olive oil and begin layering in a nonstick Bundt pan.

Cover the bottom of the pan with one layer of dough balls.

Prepare the coating mixtures. In a shallow bowl, place the provolone cheese and olives, add the basil pesto to a second bowl and add the pine nuts to a third bowl.

Roll the dough balls in the coating mixtures; then, arrange them in the Bundt pan so the various coatings are alternated. Top with Mediterranean herb mix

Cook the monkey bread in the Air Fryer at 320 degrees for 13 to 16 minutes. Bon appétit!

Fish Tacos

(Ready in about 25 minutes | Servings 3)

493 Calories; 19.2g Fat; 48.4g Carbs; 30.8g Protein; 5.8g Sugars

Ingredients

1 tablespoon mayonnaise
1 teaspoon Dijon mustard
1 tablespoon sour cream
1/2 teaspoon fresh garlic, minced
1/4 teaspoon red pepper flakes
Sea salt, to taste
2 bell peppers, seeded and sliced
1 shallot, thinly sliced
1 egg
1 tablespoon water
1 tablespoon taco seasoning mix
1/3 cup tortilla chips, crushed
1/4 cup parmesan cheese, grated
1 halibut fillets, cut into 1-inch strips
6 mini flour taco shells
6 lime wedges, for serving

Directions

Thoroughly combine the mayonnaise, mustard, sour cream, garlic, red pepper flakes, and salt. Add the bell peppers and shallots; toss to coat well. Place in your refrigerator until ready to serve.

Line the Air Fryer basket with a piece of parchment paper.

In a shallow bowl, mix the egg, water, and taco seasoning mix. In a separate shallow bowl, mix the crushed tortilla chips and parmesan.

Dip the fish into the egg mixture, then coat with the parmesan mixture, pressing to adhere.

Bake in the preheated Air Fryer at 380 degrees F for 13 minutes, flipping halfway through the cooking time.

Divide the creamed pepper mixture among the taco shells. Top with the fish, and serve with lime wedges. Enjoy!

Greek Tiganites

(Ready in about 50 minutes | Servings 3)

384 Calories; 14.1g Fat; 55.2g Carbs; 11.8g Protein; 20.5g Sugars

Ingredients

1/2 cup plain flour
1/2 cup barley flour
1 teaspoon baking powder
A pinch of salt
A pinch of sugar
A pinch of cinnamon
1 egg
1/2 cup milk
1/2 cup carbonated water
1 tablespoon butter, melted
3 tablespoons honey
3 tablespoons walnuts, chopped
3 tablespoons Greek yogurt

Directions

Thoroughly combine the flour, baking powder, salt, sugar and cinnamon in a large bowl. Fold in the egg and mix again.
Gradually pour in the milk, water and melted butter, whisking continuously, until well combined. Let the batter stand for about 30 minutes. Spritz the Air Fryer baking pan with a cooking spray. Pour the batter into the pan using a measuring cup.
Cook at 230 degrees F for 6 to 8 minutes or until golden brown. Repeat with the remaining batter.
Serve your tiganites with the honey, walnuts and Greek yogurt. Enjoy!

Air Fryer Cornbread

(Ready in about 30 minutes | Servings 4)

455 Calories; 23.9g Fat; 46.1g Carbs; 13.9g Protein; 4.7g Sugars

Ingredients

3/4 cup cornmeal
1 cup flour
2 teaspoons baking powder
1/2 tablespoon brown sugar
1/2 teaspoon salt
5 tablespoons butter, melted
3 eggs, beaten
1 cup full-fat milk

Directions

Start by preheating your Air Fryer to 370 degrees F. Then, spritz a baking pan with cooking oil.

In a mixing bowl, combine the flour, cornmeal, baking powder, brown sugar, and salt. In a separate bowl, mix the butter, eggs, and milk.

Pour the egg mixture into the dry cornmeal mixture; mix to combine well.

Pour the batter into the baking pan; cover with aluminum foil and poke tiny little holes all over the foil. Now, bake for 15 minutes. Remove the foil and bake for 10 minutes more. Transfer to a wire rack to cool slightly before cutting and serving. Bon appétit

Easy Pizza

(Ready in about 10 minutes | Servings 1)

412 Calories; 18.1g Fat; 41g Carbs; 19.8g Protein; 5.5g Sugars

Ingredients

1 (6-inch) flatbread
1 tablespoon marinara sauce
2 ounces cheddar cheese, freshly grated
1 ounce pepperoni, sliced
1/2 teaspoon dried oregano

Directions

Spread the marinara sauce over your flatbread. Add the cheese and pepperoni; sprinkle with dried oregano.
Cook your pizza at 350 degrees for 6 to 7 minutes.
Slide your pizza onto a serving plate and serve warm. Bon appétit!

Basic Air Fryer Granola

(Ready in about 45 minutes | Servings 12)

103 Calories; 6.8g Fat; 8.8g Carbs; 3.1g Protein; 3.1g Sugars

Ingredients

1/2 cup rolled oats
1 cup walnuts, chopped
3 tablespoons sunflower seeds
3 tablespoons pumpkin seeds
1 teaspoon coarse sea salt
2 tablespoons honey

Directions

Thoroughly combine all ingredients and spread the mixture onto the Air Fryer trays. Spritz with nonstick cooking spray.

Bake at 230 degrees F for 25 minutes; rotate the trays and bake 10 to 15 minutes more.

This granola can be kept in an airtight container for up to 2 weeks. Enjoy!

Puff Pastry Meat Strudel

(Ready in about 40 minutes | Servings 8)

356 Calories; 16g Fat; 35.6g Carbs; 16.5g Protein; 1.7g Sugars

Ingredients

1 tablespoon olive oil
1 small onion, chopped
2 garlic cloves, minced
1/3 pound ground beef
1/3 pound ground pork
2 tablespoons tomato puree
2 tablespoons matzo meal
Sea salt and ground black pepper, to taste
1/2 teaspoon cayenne pepper
1/4 teaspoon dried marjoram
2 cans (8-ounces) refrigerated crescent rolls
1 egg, whisked with 1 tablespoon of water
2 tablespoons sesame seeds
1/2 cup marinara sauce
1 cup sour cream

Directions

Heat the oil in a heavy skillet over medium flame. Sauté the onion just until soft and translucent. Add the garlic and sauté for 1 minute more. Add the ground beef and pork and continue to cook for 3 minutes more or until the meat is no longer pink. Remove from the heat. Add the tomato puree and matzo meal.

Roll out the puff pastry and spread the meat mixture lengthwise on the dough. Sprinkle with salt, black pepper, cayenne pepper, and marjoram. Fold in the sides of the dough over the meat mixture. Pinch the edges to seal. Place the strudel on the parchment lined Air Fryer basket. Brush the strudel with the egg wash; sprinkle with sesame seeds. Bake in the preheated Air Fryer at 330 degrees F for 18 to 20 minutes or until the pastry is puffed and golden and the filling is thoroughly cooked.

Allow your strudel to rest for 5 to 10 minutes before cutting and serving. Serve with the marinara sauce and sour cream on the side. Bon appétit!

Wontons

(Ready in about 10 minutes | Servings 2)

445 Calories; 12.7g Fat; 50.8g Carbs; 32g Protein; 2.8g Sugars

Ingredients

1/2 pound ground turkey
1 teaspoon shallot powder
1 teaspoon instant dashi granules
1 teaspoon fish sauce
1 tablespoon tomato paste
1 teaspoon soy sauce
1 teaspoon sesame oil
Seas salt and ground black pepper, to taste
20 wonton wrappers, defrosted

Directions

Brush a nonstick skillet with cooking spray. Once hot, cook the ground turkey until no longer pink, crumbling with a fork. Stir in the other ingredients, except for the wonton wrappers; stir to combine well.

Place the wonton wrappers on a clean work surface. Divide the filling between wrappers. Wet the edge of each wrapper with water, fold top half over bottom half and pinch border to seal.

Cook your wontons at 400 degrees F for 8 minutes; working in batches. Bon appétit!

Rich Couscous Salad with Goat Cheese

(Ready in about 45 minutes | Servings 4)

258 Calories; 13g Fat; 28.3g Carbs; 8.8g Protein; 8.2g Sugars

Ingredients

1/2 cup couscous
3 teaspoons olive oil
1/2 lemon, juiced, zested
1 tablespoon honey
Sea salt and freshly ground black pepper, to your liking
2 tomatoes, sliced
1 red onion, thinly sliced
1/2 English cucumber, thinly sliced
2 ounces goat cheese, crumbled
1 teaspoon ghee
2 tablespoons pine nuts
1/2 cup loosely packed Italian parsley, finely chopped

Directions

Put the couscous in a bowl; now, pour the boiling water over it. Cover and set aside for 5 to 8 minutes; fluff with a fork.
Place the couscous in a cake pan. Transfer the pan to the Air Fryer basket and cook at 360 digress F about 20 minutes. Make sure to stir every 5 minutes to ensure even cooking.
Meanwhile, in a small mixing bowl, whisk the olive oil, lemon juice and zest, honey, salt, and black pepper. Toss the couscous with this dressing. Add the tomatoes, red onion, English cucumber, and goat cheese; gently stir to combine.
Rub the ghee in the pine nuts, using your hands and place them in the Air Fryer basket. Roast for 4 minutes; give the nuts a good toss. Put the cooking basket back again and roast for a further 3 to 4 minutes. Scatter the toasted nuts over your salad and garnish with parsley. Enjoy!

Fluffy Pancake Cups with Sultanas

(Ready in about 30 minutes | Servings 3)

261 Calories; 7.7g Fat; 38g Carbs; 10g Protein; 17.2g Sugars

Ingredients

1/2 cup all-purpose flour
1/2 cup coconut flour
1/3 cup carbonated water
1/3 cup coconut milk
1 tablespoon dark rum
2 eggs
1/2 teaspoon vanilla
1/4 teaspoon cardamom
1/2 cup Sultanas, soaked for 15 minutes

Directions

In a mixing bowl, thoroughly combine the dry ingredients; in another bowl, mix the wet ingredients.
Then, stir the wet mixture into the dry mixture and stir again to combine well. Let the batter sit for 20 minutes in your refrigerator. Spoon the batter into a greased muffin tin.
Bake the pancake cups in your Air Fryer at 330 degrees F for 6 to 7 minutes or until golden brown. Repeat with the remaining batter. Bon appétit!

Hibachi-Style Fried Rice

(Ready in about 30 minutes | Servings 2)

428 Calories; 13.4g Fat; 58.9g Carbs; 14.4g Protein; 4.7g Sugars

Ingredients

1 ¾ cups leftover jasmine rice
2 teaspoons butter, melted
Sea salt and freshly ground black pepper, to your liking
2 eggs, beaten
2 scallions, white and green parts separated, chopped
1 cup snow peas
1 tablespoon Shoyu sauce
1 tablespoon sake
2 tablespoons Kewpie Japanese mayonnaise

Directions

Thoroughly combine the rice, butter, salt, and pepper in a baking dish.
Cook at 340 degrees F about 13 minutes, stirring halfway through the cooking time.
Pour the eggs over the rice and continue to cook about 5 minutes.
Next, add the scallions and snow peas and stir to combine. Continue to cook 2 to 3 minutes longer or until everything is heated through.
Meanwhile, make the sauce by whisking the Shoyu sauce, sake, and Japanese mayonnaise in a mixing bowl.
Divide the fried rice between individual bowls and serve with the prepared sauce. Enjoy!

Couscous and Black Bean Bowl

(Ready in about 35 minutes | Servings 4)

352 Calories; 12g Fat; 49.9g Carbs; 12.6g Protein; 1.7g Sugars

Ingredients

1 cup couscous
1 cup canned black beans, drained and rinsed
1 tablespoon fresh cilantro, chopped
1 bell pepper, sliced
2 tomatoes, sliced
2 cups baby spinach
1 red onion, sliced
Sea salt and ground black pepper, to taste
1 teaspoon lemon juice
1 teaspoon lemon zest
1 tablespoon olive oil
4 tablespoons tahini

Directions

Put the couscous in a bowl; pour the boiling water to cover by about 1 inch. Cover and set aside for 5 to 8 minutes; fluff with a fork.
Place the couscous in a lightly greased cake pan. Transfer the pan to the Air Fryer basket and cook at 360 digress F about 20 minutes. Make sure to stir every 5 minutes to ensure even cooking.
Transfer the prepared couscous to a mixing bowl. Add the remaining ingredients; gently stir to combine. Bon appétit!

Japanese Yaki Onigiri

(Ready in about 50 minutes | Servings 2)

603 Calories; 13.3g Fat; 95.8g Carbs; 23.3g Protein; 4.4g Sugars

Ingredients

1/2 cup sushi rice, cooked
1 cup canned green peas, drained
1/4 cup cream cheese
1/4 cup Colby cheese, shredded
2 tablespoons dashi
Salt and cracked black pepper, to taste
2 tablespoons scallions, chopped
1 cup all-purpose flour
1 egg, whisked
2 tablespoons soy sauce (unagi)

Directions

In a bowl, combine the rice, green peas, cheese, dashi, salt, black pepper, and scallions. Add the flour and egg and mix to combine well.

Refrigerate for 20 to 40 minutes.

Then, put some salt in your hands and rub to spread all around. Form the rice mixture into triangles.

Cook in the preheated Air Fryer at 370 degrees F for 7 to 10 minutes. Brush with the unagi sauce and serve immediately. Enjoy!

Aromatic Seafood Pilaf

(Ready in about 45 minutes | Servings 2)

481 Calories; 3.1g Fat; 81.5g Carbs; 29.9g Protein; 3.3g Sugars

Ingredients

1 cup jasmine rice
Salt and black pepper, to taste
1 bay leaf
1 small yellow onion, chopped
1 small garlic clove, finely chopped
1 teaspoon butter, melted
4 tablespoons cream of mushroom soup
1/2 pound shrimp, divined and sliced

Directions

Bring 2 cups of a lightly salted water to a boil in a medium saucepan over medium-high heat. Add in the jasmine rice, turn to a simmer and cook, covered, for about 18 minutes until water is absorbed.
Let the jasmine rice stand covered for 5 to 6 minutes; fluff with a fork and transfer to a lightly greased Air Fryer safe pan.
Stir in the salt, black pepper, bay leaf, yellow onion, garlic, butter and cream of mushroom soup; stir until everything is well incorporated.
Cook the rice at 350 degrees F for about 13 minutes. Stir in the shrimp and continue to cook for a further 5 minutes.
Check the rice for softness. If necessary, cook for a few minutes more. Bon appétit!

Mexican-Style Bubble Loaf

(Ready in about 20 minutes | Servings 4)

382 Calories; 17.5g Fat; 50.8g Carbs; 7.1g Protein; 6g Sugars

Ingredients

1 (16-ounce) can flaky buttermilk biscuits
4 tablespoons olive oil, melted
1/2 cup Manchego cheese, grated
1/2 teaspoon granulated garlic
1 tablespoon fresh cilantro, chopped
1/2 teaspoon Mexican oregano
1 teaspoon chili pepper flakes
Kosher salt and ground black pepper, to taste

Directions

Open a can of biscuits and cut each biscuit into quarters. Brush each piece of biscuit with the olive oil and begin layering in a lightly greased Bundt pan.

Cover the bottom of the pan with one layer of biscuits.

Next, top the first layer with half of the cheese, spices and granulated garlic. Repeat for another layer.

Finish with a third layer of dough.

Cook your bubble loaf in the Air Fryer at 330 degrees for about 15 minutes until the cheese is bubbly. Bon appétit!

Delicious Sultana Muffins

(Ready in about 20 minutes | Servings 4)

288 Calories; 9.5g Fat; 44.3g Carbs; 6.7g Protein; 18.5g Sugars

Ingredients

1 cup flour
1 teaspoon baking powder
1tablespoon honey
1 egg
1/2 teaspoon star anise, ground
1 teaspoon vanilla extract
1 egg
1/2 cup milk
2 tablespoons melted butter
1 cup dried Sultanas, soaked in
2 tablespoons of rum

Directions

Mix all the ingredients until everything is well incorporated. Spritz a silicone muffin tin with cooking spray.
Pour the batter into the silicone muffin tin.
Bake in the preheated Air Fryer at 330 degrees F for 12 to 15 minutes. Rotate the silicone muffin tin halfway through the cooking time to ensure even cooking.
Bon appétit!

Healthy Oatmeal Cups

(Ready in about 15 minutes | Servings 2)

294 Calories; 8.5g Fat; 47.2g Carbs; 10.2g Protein; 25.4g Sugars

Ingredients

1 large banana, mashed
1 cup quick-cooking steel cut oats
1 tablespoon agave syrup
1 egg, well beaten
1 cup coconut milk
3 ounces mixed berries

Directions

In a mixing bowl, thoroughly combine the banana, oats, agave syrup, beaten egg and coconut milk.
Spoon the mixture into an Air Fryer safe baking dish.
Bake in the preheated Air Fryer at 395 degrees F for about 7 minutes. Top with berries and continue to bake an additional 2 minutes.
Spoon into individual bowls and serve with a splash of coconut milk if desired. Bon appétit!

Baked Tortilla Chips

(Ready in about 15 minutes | Servings 3)

167 Calories; 6.1g Fat; 26.4g Carbs; 3.2g Protein; 0.5g Sugars

Ingredients

1/2 (12-ounce) package corn tortillas
1 tablespoon canola oil
1/2 teaspoon chili powder
1 teaspoon salt

Directions

Cut the tortillas into small rounds using a cookie cutter.
Brush the rounds with canola oil. Sprinkle them with chili powder and salt.
Transfer to the lightly greased Air Fryer basket and bake at 360 degrees F for 5 minutes, shaking the basket halfway through. Bake until the chips are crisp, working in batches.
Serve with salsa or guacamole. Enjoy!

Mexican-Style Brown Rice Casserole

(Ready in about 50 minutes | Servings 4)

433 Calories; 7.4g Fat; 79.6g Carbs; 12.1g Protein; 2.8g Sugars

Ingredients

1 tablespoon olive oil
1 shallot, chopped
2 cloves garlic, minced
1 habanero pepper, minced
2 cups brown rice
3 cups chicken broth
1 cup water
2 ripe tomatoes, pureed
Sea salt and ground black pepper, to taste
1/2 teaspoon dried Mexican oregano
1 teaspoon red pepper flakes
1 cup Mexican Cotija cheese, crumbled

Directions

In a nonstick skillet, heat the olive oil over a moderate flame. Once hot, cook the shallot, garlic, and habanero pepper until tender and fragrant; reserve. Heat the brown rice, vegetable broth and water in a pot over high heat. Bring it to a boil; turn the stove down to simmer and cook for 35 minutes. Grease a baking pan with nonstick cooking spray. Spoon the cooked rice into the baking pan. Add the sautéed mixture. Spoon the tomato puree over the sautéed mixture. Sprinkle with salt, black pepper, oregano, and red pepper.

Cook in the preheated Air Fryer at 380 degrees F for 8 minutes. Top with the Cotija cheese and bake for 5 minutes longer or until cheese is melted. Enjoy

Vegan

Fried Parsnip with Mint Yogurt Sauce

(Ready in about 10 minutes | Servings 2)

141 Calories; 2.8g Fat; 24.6g Carbs; 6.2g Protein; 8.2g Sugars

Ingredients

1/2 parsnip, peeled and sliced into sticks
1 teaspoon olive oil
Sea salt and ground black pepper, to taste
3 ounces Greek-style dairy-free yogurt, unsweetened
1 teaspoon juice
1/2 teaspoon fresh garlic, pressed
1 teaspoon fresh mint, chopped

Directions

Toss your parsnip with olive oil, salt and black pepper.
Cook the parsnip in the preheated Air Fryer at 390 degrees F for 15 minutes, shaking the basket halfway through the cooking time.
In the meantime, mix the remaining ingredients until well combined.
Serve the warm parsnip with the mint yogurt for dipping. Bon appétit!

Crispy Shawarma Chickpeas

(Ready in about 25 minutes | Servings 4)

150 Calories; 8.7g Fat; 14.2g Carbs; 4.4g Protein; 2.5g Sugars

Ingredients

1 (12-ounce) can chickpeas, drained and rinsed
2 tablespoons canola oil
1 teaspoon cayenne pepper
1 teaspoon sea salt
1 tablespoon Shawarma spice blend

Directions

Toss all ingredients in a mixing bowl.
Roast in the preheated Air Fryer at 380 degrees F for 10 minutes, shaking the basket halfway through the cooking time.
Work in batches. Bon appétit!

Potato Croquettes

(Ready in about 20 minutes | Servings 3)

171 Calories; 0.2g Fat; 38.2g Carbs; 3.3g Protein; 5.8g Sugars

Ingredients

1/2 pound sweet potatoes
1/4 cup wheat flour
1/4 cup glutinous rice flour
1 teaspoon baking powder
1 tablespoon brown sugar
1/4 teaspoon cayenne pepper
A pinch of grated nutmeg
Kosher salt and ground black pepper, to taste

Directions

Mix all ingredients in a bowl; stir until everything is well combined.
Transfer the sweet potato balls to the Air Fryer cooking basket and spritz them with a nonstick cooking oil.
Bake the sweet potato balls in the preheated Air Fryer at 360 degrees F for 15 minutes or until thoroughly cooked and crispy.
Bon appétit!

Couscous with Sun-Dried Tomatoes

(Ready in about 30 minutes | Servings 4)

230 Calories; 4.3g Fat; 41.3g Carbs; 7.2g Protein; 0.3g Sugars

Ingredients

1 cup couscous
1 cup boiled water
2 garlic cloves, pressed
1/3 cup coriander, chopped
1 cup shallots, chopped
4 ounces sun-dried tomato strips in oil
1 cup arugula lettuce, torn into pieces
2 tablespoons apple cider vinegar
Sea salt and ground black pepper, to taste

Directions

Put the couscous in a bowl; pour the boiling water, cover and set aside for 5 to 8 minutes; fluff with a fork.

Place the couscous in a lightly greased cake pan. Transfer the pan to the Air Fryer basket and cook at 360 digress F about 20 minutes. Make sure to stir every 5 minutes to ensure even cooking.

Transfer the prepared couscous to a nice salad bowl. Add the remaining ingredients; stir to combine and enjoy!

Grilled Tofu

(Ready in about 15 minutes | Servings 3)

112 Calories; 6.6g Fat; 3.6g Carbs; 12.1g Protein; 0.2g Sugars

Ingredients

8 ounces firm tofu, pressed and cut into bite-sized cubes
1 tablespoon tamari sauce
1 teaspoon peanut oil
1/2 teaspoon garlic powder
1/2 teaspoon onion powder

Directions

Toss the tofu cubes with tamari sauce, peanut oil, garlic powder and onion powder.

Cook your tofu in the preheated Air Fryer at 380 degrees F for about 13 minutes, shaking the basket once or twice to ensure even browning.

Bon appétit!

Italian-Style Tomato Cutlets

(Ready in about 10 minutes | Servings 2)

181 Calories; 2.6g Fat; 32.2g Carbs; 6.1g Protein; 4.1g Sugars

Ingredients

1 beefsteak tomato – sliced into halves
1/2 cup all-purpose flour
1/2 cup almond milk
1/2 cup breadcrumbs
1 teaspoon Italian seasoning mix

Directions

Pat the beefsteak tomato dry and set it aside.
In a shallow bowl, mix the all-purpose flour with almond milk. In another bowl, mix breadcrumbs with Italian seasoning mix.
Dip the beefsteak tomatoes in the flour mixture; then, coat the beefsteak tomatoes with the breadcrumb mixture, pressing to adhere to both sides.
Cook your tomatoes at 360 degrees F for about 5 minutes; turn them over and cook on the other side for 5 minutes longer. Serve at room temperature and enjoy!

Crispy Butternut Squash Fries

(Ready in about 25 minutes | Servings 4)

288 Calories; 7.6g Fat; 45.6g Carbs; 11.4g Protein; 3.1g Sugars

Ingredients

1 cup all-purpose flour
Salt and ground black pepper, to taste
3 tablespoons nutritional yeast flakes
1/2 cup almond milk
1/2 cup almond meal
1/2 cup bread crumbs
1 tablespoon herbs (oregano, basil, rosemary), chopped
1 pound butternut squash, peeled and cut into French fry shapes

Directions

In a shallow bowl, combine the flour, salt, and black pepper. In another shallow dish, mix the nutritional yeast flakes with the almond milk until well combined.

Mix the almond meal, breadcrumbs, and herbs in a third shallow dish. Dredge the butternut squash in the flour mixture, shaking off the excess. Then, dip in the milk mixture; lastly, dredge in the breadcrumb mixture.

Spritz the butternut squash fries with cooking oil on all sides.

Cook in the preheated Air Fryer at 400 degrees F approximately 12 minutes, turning them over halfway through the cooking time.

Serve with your favorite sauce for dipping. Bon appétit!

Granola with Raisins and Nuts

(Ready in about 40 minutes | Servings 8)

222 Calories; 14g Fat; 29.9g Carbs; 5.3g Protein; 11.3g Sugars

Ingredients

2 cups rolled oats
1/2 cup walnuts, chopped
1/3 cup almonds chopped
1/4 cup raisins
1/4 cup whole wheat pastry flour
1/2 teaspoon cinnamon
1/4 teaspoon nutmeg, preferably freshly grated
1/2 teaspoon salt
1/3 cup coconut oil, melted
1/3 cup agave nectar
1/2 teaspoon coconut extract
1/2 teaspoon vanilla extract

Directions

Thoroughly combine all ingredients. Then, spread the mixture onto the Air Fryer trays. Spritz with cooking spray.
Bake at 230 degrees F for 25 minutes; rotate the trays and bake 10 to 15 minutes more.
This granola can be stored in an airtight container for up to 2 weeks. Enjoy!

Corn on the Cob with Spicy Avocado Spread

(Ready in about 15 minutes | Servings 4)

234 Calories; 9.2g Fat; 37.9g Carbs; 7.2g Protein; 1.9g Sugars

Ingredients

4 corn cobs
1 avocado, pitted, peeled and mashed
1 clove garlic, pressed
1 tablespoon fresh lime juice
1 tablespoon soy sauce
4 teaspoons nutritional yeast
1/2 teaspoon cayenne pepper
1/2 teaspoon dried dill
Sea salt and ground black pepper, to taste
1 teaspoon hot sauce
2 heaping tablespoons fresh cilantro leaves, roughly chopped

Directions

Spritz the corn with cooking spray. Cook at 390 degrees F for 6 minutes, turning them over halfway through the cooking time.
In the meantime, mix the avocado, lime juice, soy sauce, nutritional yeast, cayenne pepper, dill, salt, black pepper, and hot sauce.
Spread the avocado mixture all over the corn on the cob. Garnish with fresh cilantro leaves. Bon appétit!

Corn on the Cob with Mediterranean Sauce

(Ready in about 10 minutes | Servings 2)

434 Calories; 27.4g Fat; 45.1g Carbs; 10.8g Protein; 5.4g Sugars

Ingredients

2 ears corn, husked
1/3 cup raw cashews, soaked
2 cloves garlic, minced
1/2 teaspoon nutritional yeast
1/2 teaspoon Dijon mustard
4 tablespoons oat milk
1 tablespoon extra-virgin olive oil
1 teaspoon freshly squeezed lemon juice
Sea salt and ground black pepper, to taste

Directions

Cook your corn in the preheated Air Fryer at 390 degrees F for about 6 minutes.

Meanwhile, blitz the remaining ingredients in your food processor or blender until smooth, creamy and uniform.

Rub each ear of corn with the Mediterranean spread and serve immediately. Bon appétit!

Green Potato Croquettes

(Ready in about 45 minutes | Servings 2)

137 Calories; 2.9g Fat; 25.2g Carbs; 4.1g Protein; 2.8g Sugars

Ingredients

1/2 pound cup russet potatoes
1 teaspoon olive oil
1/2 teaspoon garlic, pressed
2 cups loosely packed mixed greens, torn into pieces
2 tablespoons oat milk
Sea salt and ground black pepper, to taste
1/4 teaspoon red pepper flakes, crushed

Directions

Cook your potatoes for about 30 minutes until they are fork-tender; peel the potatoes and add them to a mixing bowl.
Mash your potatoes and stir in the remaining ingredients.
Shape the mixture into bite-sized balls and place them in the cooking basket; sprits the balls with a nonstick cooking oil.
Cook the croquettes at 390 degrees F for about 13 minutes, shaking the cooking basket halfway through the cooking time.
Serve with tomato ketchup if desired. Bon appétit!

Hoisin-Glazed Bok Choy

(Ready in about 10 minutes | Servings 4)

235 Calories; 11.2g Fat; 6g Carbs; 25.7g Protein; 2.2g Sugars

Ingredients

1 pound baby Bok choy, bottoms removed, leaves separated
2 garlic cloves, minced
1 teaspoon onion powder
1/2 teaspoon sage
2 tablespoons hoisin sauce
2 tablespoons sesame oil
1 tablespoon all-purpose flour

Directions

Place the Bok choy, garlic, onion powder, and sage in the lightly greased Air Fryer basket.
Cook in the preheated Air Fryer at 350 degrees F for 3 minutes.
In a small mixing dish, whisk the hoisin sauce, sesame oil, and flour.
Drizzle the sauce over the Bok choy. Cook for a further 3 minutes.
Bon appétit!

Classic Vegan Chili

(Ready in about 40 minutes | Servings 3)

335 Calories; 17.6g Fat; 37.3g Carbs; 11.5g Protein; 6.1g Sugars

Ingredients

1 tablespoon olive oil
1/2 yellow onion, chopped
2 garlic cloves, minced
2 red bell peppers, seeded and chopped
1 red chili pepper, seeded and minced
Sea salt and ground black pepper, to taste
1 teaspoon ground cumin
1 teaspoon cayenne pepper
1 teaspoon Mexican oregano
1/2 teaspoon mustard seeds
1/2 teaspoon celery seeds
1 can (28-ounces) diced tomatoes with juice
1 cup vegetable broth
1 (15-ounce) can black beans, rinsed and drained
1 bay leaf
1 teaspoon cider vinegar
1 avocado, sliced

Directions

Start by preheating your Air Fryer to 365 degrees F.

Heat the olive oil in a baking pan until sizzling. Then, sauté the onion, garlic, and peppers in the baking pan. Cook for 4 to 6 minutes. Now, add the salt, black pepper, cumin, cayenne pepper, oregano, mustard seeds, celery seeds, tomatoes, and broth. Cook for 20 minutes, stirring every 4 minutes.

Stir in the canned beans, bay leaf, cider vinegar; let it cook for a further 8 minutes, stirring halfway through the cooking time.

Serve in individual bowls garnished with the avocado slices. Enjoy!

Vegetable Fritters

(Ready in about 20 minutes | Servings 4)

299 Calories; 11.3g Fat; 44.1g Carbs; 7.9g Protein; 4.6g Sugars

Ingredients

1 pound broccoli florets
1 tablespoon ground flaxseeds
1 yellow onion, finely chopped
1 sweet pepper, seeded and chopped
1 carrot, grated
2 garlic cloves, pressed
1 teaspoon turmeric powder
1/2 teaspoon ground cumin
1/2 cup all-purpose flour
1/2 cup cornmeal
Salt and ground black pepper, to taste
2 tablespoons olive oil

Directions

Blanch the broccoli in salted boiling water until al dente, about 3 to 4 minutes. Drain well and transfer to a mixing bowl; mash the broccoli florets with the remaining ingredients.

Form the mixture into patties and place them in the lightly greased Air Fryer basket.

Cook at 400 degrees F for 6 minutes, turning them over halfway through the cooking time; work in batches.

Serve warm with your favorite Vegenaise. Enjoy!

Fried Green Beans

(Ready in about 10 minutes | Servings 2)

162 Calories; 11.3g Fat; 13g Carbs; 4.1g Protein; 6g Sugars

Ingredients

1/2 pound green beans, cleaned and trimmed
1 teaspoon extra-virgin olive oil
1/2 teaspoon onion powder
1/2 teaspoon shallot powder
1/4 teaspoon cumin powder
1/2 teaspoon cayenne pepper
1/2 teaspoon garlic powder
Himalayan salt and freshly ground black pepper, to taste
1 tablespoon lime juice
1 tablespoon soy sauce
1/4 cup pecans, roughly chopped

Directions

Toss the green beans with olive oil, spices and lime juice.
Cook the green beans in your Air Fryer at 400 degrees F for 5 minutes, shaking the basket halfway through the cooking time to promote even cooking.
Toss the green beans with soy sauce and serve garnished with chopped pecans. Bon appétit!

Portobello Mushroom Schnitzel

(Ready in about 10 minutes | Servings 2)

156 Calories; 1.4g Fat; 27.1g Carbs; 7.2g Protein; 5g Sugars

Ingredients

7 ounces Portobello mushrooms
1/4 cup chickpea flour
1/4 cup plain flour
1/3 cup beer
1 cup breadcrumbs
1/2 teaspoon porcini powder
1/2 teaspoon dried basil
1/4 teaspoon dried oregano
1/4 teaspoon ground cumin
1/4 teaspoon ground bay leaf
1/2 teaspoon garlic powder
1/2 teaspoon shallot powder
Kosher salt and ground black pepper, to taste

Directions

Pat dry the Portobello mushrooms and set them aside.
Then, add the flour and beer to a rimmed plate and mix to combine well. In another bowl, mix the breadcrumbs with spices.
Dip your mushrooms in the flour mixture, then, coat them with the breadcrumb mixture.
Cook the breaded mushrooms in the preheated Air Fryer at 380 degrees F for 6 to 7 minutes, flipping them over halfway through the cooking time. Eat warm.

Herb Roasted Potatoes and Peppers

(Ready in about 30 minutes | Servings 4)

158 Calories; 6.8g Fat; 22.6g Carbs; 1.8g Protein; 2.2g Sugars

Ingredients

1 pound russet potatoes, cut into 1-inch chunks
2 bell peppers, seeded and cut into 1-inch chunks
2 tablespoons olive oil
1 teaspoon dried rosemary
1 teaspoon dried basil
1 teaspoon dried oregano
1 teaspoon dried parsley flakes
Sea salt and ground black pepper, to taste
1/2 teaspoon smoked paprika

Directions

Toss all ingredients in the Air Fryer basket.
Roast at 400 degrees F for 15 minutes, tossing the basket occasionally. Work in batches.
Serve warm and enjoy!

Spicy Bean Burgers

(Ready in about 15 minutes | Servings 3)

227 Calories; 2.3g Fat; 40.1g Carbs; 12.1g Protein; 2.2g Sugars

Ingredients

1/2 cup old-fashioned oats
2 tablespoons red onions, finely chopped
2 garlic cloves, finely chopped
8 ounces canned beans
1/3 cup marinara sauce
1 teaspoon tamari sauce
A few drops of liquid smoke
Kosher salt and ground black pepper, to taste
1/4 teaspoon ancho chile powder

Directions

Pulse all ingredients in your food processor leaving some larger chunks of beans.
Now, form the mixture into patties and place them in the Air Fryer cooking basket. Brush the patties with a nonstick cooking oil.
Cook your burgers at 380 degrees F for about 15 minutes, flipping them halfway through the cooking time.
Serve on burger buns garnished with your favorite fixings. Bon appétit!

Potato Chips with Vegveeta Dip

(Ready in about 1 hour | Servings 4)

244 Calories; 18g Fat; 19.4g Carbs; 4g Protein; 1.7g Sugars

Ingredients

1 large potato, cut into 1/8 inch thick slices
1 tablespoon olive oil
Sea salt, to taste
1/2 teaspoon red pepper flakes, crushed
1 teaspoon fresh rosemary
1/2 teaspoon fresh sage
1/2 teaspoon fresh basil Dipping Sauce:
1/3 cup raw cashews
1 tablespoon tahini
1 ½ tablespoons olive oil
1/4 cup raw almonds
1/4 teaspoon prepared yellow mustard

Directions

Soak the potatoes in a large bowl of cold water for 20 to 30 minutes. Drain the potatoes and pat them dry with a kitchen towel.
Toss with olive oil and seasonings.
Place in the lightly greased cooking basket and cook at 380 degrees F for 30 minutes. Work in batches.
Meanwhile, puree the sauce ingredients in your food processor until smooth. Serve the potato chips with the Vegveeta sauce for dipping. Bon appétit!

Italian-Style Risi e Bisi

(Ready in about 20 minutes | Servings 4)

434 Calories; 8.3g Fat; 79.8g Carbs; 9.9g Protein; 5g Sugars

Ingredients

1 cups brown rice
4 cups water
1/2 cup frozen green peas
3 tablespoons soy sauce
1 tablespoon olive oil
1 cup brown mushrooms, sliced
2 garlic cloves, minced
1 small-sized onion, chopped
1 tablespoon fresh parsley, chopped

Directions

Heat the brown rice and water in a pot over high heat. Bring it to a boil; turn the stove down to simmer and cook for 35 minutes. Allow your rice to cool completely.

Transfer the cold cooked rice to the lightly greased Air Fryer pan. Add the remaining ingredients and stir to combine.

Cook in the preheated Air Fryer at 360 degrees F for 18 to 22 minutes. Serve warm.

The Best Crispy Tofu

(Ready in about 55 minutes | Servings 4)

245 Calories; 13.3g Fat; 16.7g Carbs; 18.2g Protein; 1.2g Sugars

Ingredients

16 ounces firm tofu, pressed and cubed
1 tablespoon vegan oyster sauce
1 tablespoon tamari sauce
1 teaspoon cider vinegar
1 teaspoon pure maple syrup
1 teaspoon sriracha
1/2 teaspoon shallot powder
1/2 teaspoon porcini powder
1 teaspoon garlic powder
1 tablespoon sesame oil
5 tablespoons cornstarch

Directions

Toss the tofu with the oyster sauce, tamari sauce, vinegar, maple syrup, sriracha, shallot powder, porcini powder, garlic powder, and sesame oil. Let it marinate for 30 minutes.

Toss the marinated tofu with the cornstarch.

Cook at 360 degrees F for 10 minutes; turn them over and cook for 12 minutes more. Bon appétit!

Mashed Potatoes with Roasted Peppers

(Ready in about 1 hour | Servings 4)

490 Calories; 17g Fat; 79.1g Carbs; 10.5g Protein; 9.8g Sugars

Ingredients

4 potatoes
1 tablespoon vegan margarine
1 teaspoon garlic powder
1 pound bell peppers, seeded and quartered lengthwise
2 Fresno peppers, seeded and halved lengthwise
4 tablespoons olive oil
2 tablespoons cider vinegar
4 garlic cloves, pressed
Kosher salt, to taste
1/2 teaspoon freshly ground black pepper
1/2 teaspoon dried dill

Directions

Place the potatoes in the Air Fryer basket and cook at 400 degrees F for 40 minutes. Discard the skin and mash the potatoes with the vegan margarine and garlic powder.

Then, roast the peppers at 400 degrees F for 5 minutes. Give the peppers a half turn; place them back in the cooking basket and roast for another 5 minutes.

Turn them one more time and roast until the skin is charred and soft or 5 more minutes. Peel the peppers and let them cool to room temperature.

Toss your peppers with the remaining ingredients and serve with the mashed potatoes. Bon appétit!

Paprika Squash Fries

(Ready in about 15 minutes | Servings 3)

202 Calories; 5.8g Fat; 30.2g Carbs; 8.1g Protein; 2.9g Sugars

Ingredients

1/4 cup rice milk
1/4 cup almond flour
2 tablespoons nutritional yeast
1/4 teaspoon shallot powder
1/2 teaspoon garlic powder
1/2 teaspoon paprika
Sea salt and ground black pepper, to taste
1 pound butternut squash, peeled and into sticks
1 cup tortilla chips, crushed

Directions

In a bowl, thoroughly combine the milk flour, nutritional yeast and spices. In another shallow bowl, place the crushed tortilla chips.
Dip the butternut squash sticks into the batter and then, roll them over the crushed tortilla chips until well coated.
Arrange the squash pieces in the Air Fryer cooking basket. Cook the squash fries at 400 degrees F for about 12 minutes, shaking the basket once or twice. Bon appétit!

Baked Spicy Tortilla Chips

(Ready in about 20 minutes | Servings 3)

189 Calories; 5.1g Fat; 30.7g Carbs; 4.7g Protein; 2g Sugars

Ingredients

6 (6-inch) corn tortillas
1 teaspoon canola oil
1 teaspoon salt
1/4 teaspoon ground white pepper
1/2 teaspoon ground cumin
1/2 teaspoon ancho chili powder

Directions

Slice the tortillas into quarters. Brush the tortilla pieces with the canola oil until well coated.
Toss with the spices and transfer to the Air Fryer basket.
Bake at 360 degrees F for 8 minutes or until lightly golden. Work in batches. Bon appétit!

Authentic Churros with Hot Chocolate

(Ready in about 25 minutes | Servings 3)

432 Calories; 15.8g Fat; 63.9g Carbs; 8.4g Protein; 24.7g Sugars

Ingredients

1/2 cup water
2 tablespoons granulated sugar
1/4 teaspoon sea salt
1 teaspoon lemon zest
1 tablespoon canola oil
1 cup all-purpose flour
2 ounces dark chocolate
1 cup milk
1 tablespoon cornstarch
1/3 cup sugar
1 teaspoon ground cinnamon

Directions

To make the churro dough, boil the water in a pan over medium-high heat; now, add the sugar, salt and lemon zest; cook until dissolved.

Add the canola oil and remove the pan from the heat. Gradually stir in the flour, whisking continuously until the mixture forms a ball.

Pour the mixture into a piping bag with a large star tip. Squeeze 4-inch strips of dough into the greased Air Fryer pan.

Cook at 410 degrees F for 6 minutes.

Meanwhile, prepare the hot chocolate for dipping. Melt the chocolate and 1/2 cup of milk in a pan over low heat.

Dissolve the cornstarch in the remaining 1/2 cup of milk; stir into the hot chocolate mixture.

Cook on low heat approximately 5 minutes.

Mix the sugar and cinnamon; roll the churros in this mixture. Serve with the hot chocolate on the side. Enjoy!

Dessert

Chocolate Banana Crepes

(Ready in about 30 minutes | Servings 2)

214 Calories; 5.4g Fat; 36.4g Carbs; 5.8g Protein; 25.1g Sugars

Ingredients

1 small ripe banana
1/8 teaspoon baking powder
1/4 cup chocolate chips
1 egg, whisked

Directions

Mix all ingredients until creamy and fluffy. Let it stand for about 20 minutes.
Spritz the Air Fryer baking pan with cooking spray. Pour 1/2 of the batter into the pan using a measuring cup.
Cook at 230 degrees F for 4 to 5 minutes or until golden brown.
Repeat with another crepe. Bon appétit!

French Toast with Blackberries

(Ready in about 20 minutes | Servings 2)

324 Calories; 14.9g Fat; 42.2g Carbs; 6.5g Protein; 24.9g Sugars

Ingredients

1 tablespoons butter, at room temperature
1 egg
2 tablespoons granulated sugar
1/4 teaspoon ground cinnamon
1/4 teaspoon vanilla extract
6 slices French baguette
1 cup fresh blackberries
2 tablespoons powdered sugar

Direction

Start by preheating your Air Fryer to 375 degrees F.
In a mixing dish, whisk the butter, egg, granulated sugar, cinnamon and vanilla.
Dip all the slices of the French baguette in this mixture. Transfer the French toast to the baking pan.
Bake in the preheated Air Fryer for 8 minutes, turning them over halfway through the cooking time to ensure even cooking.
To serve, divide the French toast between two warm plates. Arrange the blackberries on top of each slice. Dust with powdered sugar and serve immediately. Enjoy!

Chocolate Peppermint Cream Pie

(Ready in about 40 minutes + chilling time | Servings 4)

417 Calories; 28.2g Fat; 39g Carbs; 3.3g Protein; 23g Sugars

Ingredients

12 cookies, crushed into fine crumbs
2 ounces butter, melted
2 ounces dark chocolate chunks
1/2 cup heavy whipping cream
4 tablespoons brown sugar
2 drops peppermint extract
1/4 teaspoon ground cinnamon
1/4 teaspoon ground cloves

Directions

In a mixing bowl, thoroughly combine crushed cookies and butter to make the crust. Press the crust into the bottom of a lightly oiled baking dish.

Bake the crust at 350 degrees F for 18 minutes. Transfer it to your freezer for 20 minutes.

Then, microwave the chocolate chunks for 30 seconds; stir in the heavy whipping cream, brown sugar, peppermint extract, cinnamon and cloves.

Spread the mousse evenly over the crust. Refrigerate until firm for about 3 hours.

Bon appétit!

Apple Crisp

(Ready in about 40 minutes | Servings 4)

403 Calories; 18.6g Fat; 61.5g Carbs; 2.9g Protein; 40.2g Sugars

Ingredients

4 cups apples, peeled, cored and sliced
1/2 cup brown sugar
1 tablespoon honey
1 tablespoon cornmeal
1/4 teaspoon ground cloves
1/2 teaspoon ground cinnamon
1/4 cup water
1/2 cup quick-cooking oats
1/2 cup all-purpose flour
1/2 cup caster sugar
1/2 teaspoon baking powder
1/3 cup coconut oil, melted

Directions

Toss the sliced apples with the brown sugar, honey, cornmeal, cloves, and cinnamon. Divide between four custard cups coated with cooking spray.

In a mixing dish, thoroughly combine the remaining ingredients. Sprinkle over the apple mixture.

Bake in the preheated Air Fryer at 330 degrees F for 35 minutes. Bon appétit!

Cake with Walnuts

(Ready in about 20 minutes | Servings 4)

455 Calories; 25.4g Fat; 52.1g Carbs; 6.1g Protein; 15g Sugars

Ingredients

1 (10-ounces) can crescent rolls
1/2 stick butter
1/2 cup caster sugar
1 teaspoon pumpkin pie spice blend
1 tablespoon dark rum
1/2 cup walnuts, chopped

Directions

Start by preheating your Air Fryer to 350 degrees F.
Roll out the crescent rolls. Spread the butter onto the crescent rolls; scatter the sugar, spices and walnuts over the rolls. Drizzle with rum and roll them up.
Using your fingertips, gently press them to seal the edges.
Bake your cake for about 13 minutes or until the top is golden brown. Bon appétit!

Fruit Kabobs

(Ready in about 10 minutes | Servings 6)

165 Calories; 0.7g Fat; 41.8g Carbs; 1.6g Protein; 33.6g Sugars

Ingredients

2 pears, diced into bite-sized chunks
2 apples, diced into bite-sized chunks
2 mangos, diced into bite-sized chunks
1 tablespoon fresh lemon juice
1 teaspoon vanilla essence
2 tablespoons maple syrup
1 teaspoon ground cinnamon
1/2 teaspoon ground cloves

Directions

Toss all ingredients in a mixing dish.
Tread the fruit pieces on skewers.
Cook at 350 degrees F for 5 minutes. Bon appétit!

Cinnamon Dough Dippers

(Ready in about 20 minutes | Servings 6)

332 Calories; 14.8g Fat; 45.6g Carbs; 5.1g Protein; 27.6g Sugars

Ingredients

1/2 pound bread dough
1/4 cup butter, melted
1/2 cup caster sugar
1 tablespoon cinnamon
1/2 cup cream cheese, softened
1 cup powdered sugar
1/2 teaspoon vanilla
2 tablespoons milk

Directions

Roll the dough into a log; cut into 1-1/2 inch strips using a pizza cutter.

Mix the butter, sugar, and cinnamon in a small bowl. Use a rubber spatula to spread the butter mixture over the tops of the dough dippers.

Bake at 360 degrees F for 7 to 8 minutes, turning them over halfway through the cooking time. Work in batches.

Meanwhile, make the glaze dip by whisking the remaining ingredients with a hand mixer. Beat until a smooth consistency is reached.

Serve at room temperature and enjoy!

Sweet Dough Dippers

(Ready in about 10 minutes | Servings 4)

255 Calories; 7.6g Fat; 42.1g Carbs; 5g Protein; 17.1g Sugars

Ingredients

8 ounces bread dough
2 tablespoons butter, melted
2 ounces powdered sugar

Directions

Cut the dough into strips and twist them together 3 to 4 times. Then, brush the dough twists with melted butter and sprinkle sugar over them.
Cook the dough twists at 350 degrees F for 8 minutes, tossing the basket halfway through the cooking time.
Serve with your favorite dip. Bon appétit!

Banana Chips with Chocolate Glaze

(Ready in about 20 minutes | Servings 2)

201 Calories; 7.5g Fat; 37.1g Carbs; 1.8g Protein; 22.9g Sugars

Ingredients

2 banana, cut into slices
1/4 teaspoon lemon zest
1 tablespoon agave syrup
1 tablespoon cocoa powder
1 tablespoon coconut oil, melted

Directions

Toss the bananas with the lemon zest and agave syrup. Transfer your bananas to the parchmentlined cooking basket.

Bake in the preheated Air Fryer at 370 degrees F for 12 minutes, turning them over halfway through the cooking time.

In the meantime, melt the coconut oil in your microwave; add the cocoa powder and whisk to combine well.

Serve the baked banana chips with a few drizzles of the chocolate glaze. Enjoy!

Air Grilled Apricots with Mascarpone

(Ready in about 30 minutes | Servings 2)

244 Calories; 10.9g Fat; 30.1g Carbs; 7.5g Protein; 28.1g Sugars

Ingredients

6 apricots, halved and pitted
1 teaspoon coconut oil, melted
2 ounces mascarpone cheese
1/2 teaspoon vanilla extract
1 tablespoon confectioners' sugar
A pinch of sea salt

Directions

Place the apricots in the Air Fryer cooking basket. Drizzle the apricots with melted coconut oil.

Cook the apricots at 320 degrees F for about 25 minutes or until the top is golden.

In a bowl, whisk the mascarpone, vanilla extract, confectioners' sugar by hand until soft and creamy.

Remove the apricots from the cooking basket. Spoon the whipped mascarpone into the cavity of each apricot.

Sprinkle with coarse sea salt and enjoy!

Chocolate Cake

(Ready in about 35 minutes + chilling time | Servings 6)

689 Calories; 43.4g Fat; 76.1g Carbs; 6.5g Protein; 55.6g Sugars

Ingredients

2 eggs, beaten
2/3 cup sour cream
1 cup flour
1/2 cup sugar
1/4 cup honey
1/3 cup coconut oil, softened
1/4 cup cocoa powder
2 tablespoons chocolate chips
1 ½ teaspoons baking powder
1 teaspoon vanilla extract
1/2 teaspoon pure rum extract
Chocolate Frosting:
1/2 cup butter, softened
1/4 cup cocoa powder
2 cups powdered sugar
2 tablespoons milk

Directions

Mix all ingredients for the chocolate cake with a hand mixer on low speed. Scrape the batter into a cake pan. Bake at 330 degrees F for 25 to 30 minutes. Transfer the cake to a wire rack

Meanwhile, whip the butter and cocoa until smooth. Stir in the powdered sugar. Slowly and gradually, pour in the milk until your frosting reaches desired consistency.

Whip until smooth and fluffy; then, frost the cooled cake. Place in your refrigerator for a couple of hours. Serve well chilled.

Swedish Kärleksmums

(Ready in about 20 minutes | Servings 3)

256 Calories; 11.5g Fat; 27.6g Carbs; 5.1g Protein; 13.9g Sugars

Ingredients

1 tablespoons Swedish butter, at room temperature
4 tablespoons brown sugar
1 egg
1 tablespoon lingonberry jam
5 tablespoons all-purpose flour
1/2 teaspoon baking powder
2 tablespoons cocoa powder
A pinch of grated nutmeg
A pinch of coarse sea salt

Directions

Cream the butter and sugar using an electric mixer. Fold in the egg and lingonberry jam and mix to combine well.

Stir in the flour, baking powder, cocoa powder, grated nutmeg and salt; mix again to combine well. Pour the batter into a lightly buttered baking pan.

Bake your cake at 330 degrees F for about 15 minutes until a tester inserted into the center of the cake comes out dry and clean. Bon appétit!

Chocolate and Coconut Cake

(Ready in about 20 minutes | Servings 10)

252 Calories; 18.9g Fat; 17.9g Carbs; 3.4g Protein; 13.8g Sugars

Ingredients

1 stick butter
1 ¼ cups dark chocolate, broken into chunks
1/4 cup tablespoon agave syrup
1/4 cup sugar
2 tablespoons milk
2 eggs, beaten
1/3 cup coconut, shredded

Directions

Begin by preheating your Air Fryer to 330 degrees F.
In a microwave-safe bowl, melt the butter, chocolate, and agave syrup. Allow it to cool to room temperature.
Add the remaining ingredients to the chocolate mixture; stir to combine well. Scrape the batter into a lightly greased baking pan. Bake in the preheated Air Fryer for 15 minutes or until a toothpick comes out dry and clean. Enjoy!

Chocolate Raspberry Wontons

(Ready in about 15 minutes | Servings 6)

356 Calories; 13g Fat; 51.2g Carbs; 7.9g Protein; 11.3g Sugars

Ingredients

1 (12-ounce) package wonton wrappers
6 ounces chocolate chips
1/2 cup raspberries, mashed
1 egg, lightly whisked + 1 tablespoon of water (egg wash)
1/4 cup caster sugar

Directions

Divide the chocolate chips and raspberries among the wonton wrappers. Now, fold the wrappers diagonally in half over the filling; press the edges with a fork.
Brush with the egg wash and seal the edges.
Bake at 370 degrees F for 8 minutes, flipping them halfway through the cooking time.
Work in batches. Sprinkle the caster sugar over your wontons and enjoy!

Classic Brownie Cupcakes

(Ready in about 25 minutes | Servings 3)

264 Calories; 17.7g Fat; 24.4g Carbs; 4.6g Protein; 10.9g Sugars

Ingredients

1/3 cup all-purpose flour
1/4 teaspoon baking powder
3 tablespoons cocoa powder
1/3 cup caster sugar
2 ounces butter, room temperature
1 large egg
1/2 teaspoon rum extract
A pinch of ground cinnamon
A pinch of salt

Directions

Mix the dry ingredients in a bowl. In another bowl, mix the wet ingredients. Gradually, stir in the wet ingredients into the dry mixture.

Divide the batter among muffin cups and transfer them to the Air Fryer cooking basket.

Bake your cupcakes at 330 degrees for 15 minuets until a tester comes out dry and clean.

Transfer to a wire rack and let your cupcakes sit for 10 minutes before unmolding. Bon appétit!

Easy Blueberry Muffins

(Ready in about 20 minutes | Servings 10)

191 Calories; 8g Fat; 25.7g Carbs; 4.3g Protein; 10.9g Sugars

Ingredients

1 ½ cups all-purpose flour
1/2 teaspoon baking soda
1 teaspoon baking powder
1/4 teaspoon kosher salt
1/2 cup granulated sugar
2 eggs, whisked
1/2 cup milk
1/4 cup coconut oil, melted
1/2 teaspoon vanilla paste
1 cup fresh blueberries

Directions

In a mixing bowl, combine the flour, baking soda, baking powder, sugar, and salt. Whisk to combine well.

In another mixing bowl, mix the eggs, milk, coconut oil, and vanilla.

Now, add the wet egg mixture to dry the flour mixture. Then, carefully fold in the fresh blueberries; gently stir to combine.

Scrape the batter mixture into the muffin cups. Bake your muffins at 350 degrees F for 12 minutes or until the tops are golden brown.

Sprinkle some extra icing sugar over the top of each muffin if desired. Serve and enjoy!

Classic Butter Cake

(Ready in about 35 minutes | Servings 8)

244 Calories; 14.2g Fat; 25.1g Carbs; 4.2g Protein; 12.8g Sugars

Ingredients

1 stick butter, at room temperature
1 cup sugar
2 eggs
1 cup all-purpose flour
1 teaspoon baking powder
1/2 teaspoon baking soda
1/4 teaspoon salt
A pinch of freshly grated nutmeg
A pinch of ground star anise
1/4 cup buttermilk
1 teaspoon vanilla essence

Directions

Begin by preheating your Air Fryer to 320 degrees F. Spritz the bottom and sides of a baking pan with cooking spray.
Beat the butter and sugar with a hand mixer until creamy. Then, fold in the eggs, one at a time, and mix well until fluffy.
Stir in the flour along with the remaining ingredients. Mix to combine well. Scrape the batter into the prepared baking pan.
Bake for 15 minutes; rotate the pan and bake an additional 15 minutes, until the top of the cake springs back when gently pressed with your fingers. Bon appétit!

Baked Fruit Salad

(Ready in about 15 minutes | Servings 2)

263 Calories; 7.3g Fat; 53.2g Carbs; 1.3g Protein; 37.7g Sugars

Ingredients

1 banana, peeled
1 cooking pear, cored
1 cooking apple, cored
1 tablespoon freshly squeezed lemon juice
1/2 teaspoon ground star anise
1/4 teaspoon ground cinnamon
1/2 teaspoon granulated ginger
1/4 cup brown sugar
1 tablespoon coconut oil, melted

Directions

Toss your fruits with lemon juice, star anise, cinnamon, ginger, sugar and coconut oil.
Transfer the fruits to the Air Fryer cooking basket.
Bake the fruit salad in the preheated Air Fryer at 330 degrees F for 15 minutes.
Serve in individual bowls, garnished with vanilla ice cream. Bon appétit!

Cinnamon Dough Dippers

(Ready in about 20 minutes | Servings 6)

332 Calories; 14.8g Fat; 45.6g Carbs; 5.1g Protein; 27.6g Sugars

Ingredients

1/2 pound bread dough
1/4 cup butter, melted
1/2 cup caster sugar
1 tablespoon cinnamon
1/2 cup cream cheese, softened
3 cup powdered sugar
1/2 teaspoon vanilla
4 tablespoons milk

Directions

Roll the dough into a log; cut into 1-1/2 inch strips using a pizza cutter.
Mix the butter, sugar, and cinnamon in a small bowl. Use a rubber spatula to spread the butter mixture over the tops of the dough dippers.
Bake at 360 degrees F for 7 to 8 minutes, turning them over halfway through the cooking time. Work in batches.
Meanwhile, make the glaze dip by whisking the remaining ingredients with a hand mixer. Beat until a smooth consistency is reached.
Serve at room temperature and enjoy!

Perfect English-Style Scones

(Ready in about 15 minutes | Servings 4)

458 Calories; 25g Fat; 47.1g Carbs; 6.8g Protein; 7.9g Sugars

Ingredients

1 ½ cups cake flour
1/4 cup caster sugar
1 teaspoon baking powder
1 teaspoon baking soda
1/4 teaspoon salt
1/2 teaspoon vanilla essence
1/2 stick butter
1 egg, beaten
1/2 cup almond milk

Directions

Start by preheating your Air Fryer to 360 degrees F.

Thoroughly combine all dry ingredients. In another bowl, combine all wet ingredients. Then, add the wet mixture to the dry ingredients and stir to combine well.

Roll your dough out into a circle and cut into wedges.

Bake the scones in the preheated Air Fryer for about 11 minutes, flipping them halfway through the cooking time. Bon appétit!

Fried Honey Banana

(Ready in about 20 minutes | Servings 2)

363 Calories; 14.3g Fat; 61.1g Carbs; 3.7g Protein; 33.3g Sugars

Ingredients

1 ripe bananas, peeled and sliced
2 tablespoons honey
3 tablespoons rice flour
3 tablespoons desiccated coconut
A pinch of fine sea salt
1/2 teaspoon baking powder
1/4 teaspoon cardamom powder

Directions

Preheat the Air Fryer to 390 degrees F.
Drizzle honey over the banana slices.
In a mixing dish, thoroughly combine the rice flour, coconut, salt, baking powder, and cardamom powder. Roll each slice of banana over the flour mixture.
Bake in the preheated Air Fryer approximately 13 minutes, flipping them halfway through the cooking time. Bon appétit!

Mini Apple and Cranberry Crisp Cakes

(Ready in about 40 minutes | Servings 3)

338 Calories; 17.5g Fat; 41.9g Carbs; 5.2g Protein; 18.1g Sugars

Ingredients

2 Bramley cooking apples, peeled, cored and chopped
1/4 cup dried cranberries
1 teaspoon fresh lemon juice
1 tablespoon golden caster sugar
1 teaspoon apple pie spice mix
A pinch of coarse salt
1/2 cup rolled oats
1/3 cup brown bread crumbs
1/4 cup butter, diced

Directions

Divide the apples and cranberries between three lightly greased ramekins. Drizzle your fruits with lemon juice and sprinkle with caster sugar, spice mix and salt.

Then, make the streusel by mixing the remaining ingredients in a bowl. Spread the streusel batter on top of the filling.

Bake the mini crisp cakes in the preheated Air Fryer at 330 degrees F for 35 minutes or until they're a dark golden brown around the edges.

Bon appétit!

Grilled Banana Boats

(Ready in about 15 minutes | Servings 3)

269 Calories; 5.9g Fat; 47.9g Carbs; 2.6g Protein; 28.3g Sugars

Ingredients

3 large bananas
1 tablespoon ginger snaps
2 tablespoons mini chocolate chips
3 tablespoons mini marshmallows
3 tablespoons crushed vanilla wafers

Directions

In the peel, slice your banana lengthwise; make sure not to slice all the way through the banana. Divide the remaining ingredients between the banana pockets.

Place in the Air Fryer grill pan. Cook at 395 degrees F for 7 minutes. Let the banana boats cool for 5 to 6 minutes, and then eat with a spoon. Bon appétit!

Coconut Cheesecake Bites

(Ready in about 25 minutes + chilling time | Servings 8)

415 Calories; 32.3g Fat; 26.4g Carbs; 6.8g Protein; 17.1g Sugars

Ingredients

1 ½ cups Oreo cookies, crushed
4 ounces granulated sugar
4 tablespoons butter, softened
12 ounces cream cheese
4 ounces double cream
2 eggs, lightly whisked
1 teaspoon pure vanilla extract
1 teaspoon pure coconut extract
1 cup toasted coconut

Directions

Start by preheating your Air Fryer to 350 degrees F.
Mix the crushed Oreos with sugar and butter; press the crust into silicone cupcake molds. Bake for 5 minutes and allow them to cool on wire racks.
Using an electric mixer, whip the cream cheese and double cream until fluffy; add one egg at a time and continue to beat until creamy. Finally, add the vanilla and coconut extract.
Pour the topping mixture on top of the crust. Bake at 320 degrees F for 13 to 15 minutes.
Afterwards, top with the toasted coconut. Allow the mini cheesecakes to chill in your refrigerator before serving. Bon appétit!

Other Air Fryer Recipes

Simple Turkey Meatballs

(Ready in about 35 minutes | Servings 4)

327 Calories; 18.7g Fat; 6.9g Carbs; 32.2g Protein; 1.7g Sugars

Ingredients

½ pounds ground turkey
1/2 cup parmesan cheese, grated
1/2 cup tortilla chips, crumbled
1 yellow onion, finely chopped
2 tablespoons Italian parsley, finely chopped
1 egg, beaten
2 cloves garlic, minced
1 tablespoon soy sauce
1 teaspoon Italian seasoning mix
1 teaspoon olive oil

Directions

Thoroughly combine all of the above ingredients until well incorporated. Shape the mixture into 10 equal meatballs.
Spritz a cooking basket with a nonstick cooking spray. Cook at 360 degrees F for about 10 minutes or to your desired degree of doneness.

Pork and Rice Casserole

(Ready in about 45 minutes | Servings 5)

506 Calories; 34.7g Fat; 13.4g Carbs; 34.7g Protein; 2.3g Sugars

Ingredients

1 teaspoon olive oil
1 small-sized yellow onion, chopped
1 pound ground pork (84% lean)
Salt and black pepper, to taste
1/2 cups cooked wild rice, uncooked
1/2 cup cream of mushroom soup
1/2 tomato paste
1 jalapeno pepper, minced
1 teaspoon Italian spice mix
1/2 cup Asiago cheese, shredded

Directions

Start by preheating your Air Fryer to 350 degrees F.
Heat the olive oil in a nonstick over medium-high heat. Then, sauté the onion and ground pork for 6 to 7 minutes, crumbling with a spatula. Season with salt and black pepper to your liking.
Spoon the pork mixture into a lightly greased baking dish.
Spoon the cooked rice over the pork layer. In a mixing dish, thoroughly combine the remaining ingredients.
Bake for 15 minutes or until bubbly and heated through.

Paprika Steak with Cauliflower

(Ready in about 40 minutes | Servings 5)

196 Calories; 7.8g Fat; 7.5g Carbs; 25.4g Protein; 2.8g Sugars

Ingredients

1 pound Porterhouse steak, sliced
1 teaspoon butter, room temperature
Coarse sea salt and ground black pepper, to taste
1/2 teaspoon shallot powder
1/2 teaspoon porcini powder
1 teaspoon granulated garlic
1 teaspoon smoked paprika
1 pound cauliflower, torn into florets

Directions

Brush the steak with butter on all sides; season it with all spices. Season the cauliflower with salt and pepper to taste.
Place the steak in the cooking basket and roast at 400 degrees F for 12 minutes; turn over halfway through the cooking time.
Remove the cauliflower from the basket and continue to cook your steak for 2 to 3 minutes if needed.
Serve the steak garnished with the cauliflower. Eat warm.

Salmon with Fennel Scent

(Ready in about 25 minutes | Servings 4)

306 Calories; 16.3g Fat; 5.6g Carbs; 32.2g Protein; 3g Sugars

Ingredients

1 pound salmon
1 fennel, quartered
1 teaspoon olive oil
Sea salt and ground black pepper, to taste
1/2 teaspoon paprika
1 tablespoon balsamic vinegar
1 tablespoon lime juice
1 tablespoon extra-virgin olive oil
1 tomato, sliced
1 cucumber, sliced
1 tablespoon sesame seeds, lightly toasted

Directions

Toss the salmon and fennel with 1 teaspoon of olive oil, salt, black pepper and paprika.
Cook in the preheated Air Fryer at 380 degrees F for 12 minutes; shaking the basket once or twice.
Cut the salmon into bite-sized strips and transfer them to a nice salad bowl. Add in the fennel, balsamic vinegar, lime juice, 1 tablespoon of extra-virgin olive oil, tomato and cucumber.
Toss to combine well and serve garnished with lightly toasted sesame seeds.

Broccoli and Cauliflower in Tahini Sauce

(Ready in about 20 minutes | Servings 4)

178 Calories; 11.9g Fat; 14.6g Carbs; 6.8g Protein; 4.8g Sugars

Ingredients

1/2 pound broccoli, broken into florets
1/2 pound cauliflower, broken into florets
1 teaspoon onion powder
1/2 teaspoon porcini powder
1/4 teaspoon cumin powder
1/2 teaspoon granulated garlic
1 teaspoon olive oil
3 tablespoons tahini
2 tablespoons soy sauce
1 teaspoon white vinegar
Salt and chili flakes, to taste

Directions

Start by preheating your Air Fryer to 400 degrees F.
Now, toss the vegetables with the onion powder, porcini powder cumin powder, garlic and olive oil. Transfer your vegetables to the lightly greased cooking basket.
Air Fry your veggies in the preheated Air Fryer at 400 degrees F for 6 minutes. Remove the broccoli florets from the cooking basket.
Continue to cook the cauliflower for 5 to 6 minutes more.
Meanwhile, make the tahini sauce by simply whisking the remaining ingredients in a small bowl. Spoon the sauce over the warm vegetables and serve immediately.

Vegetables in Chips with Mayonnaise

(Ready in about 25 minutes | Servings 5)

187 Calories; 11.2g Fat; 20.1g Carbs; 2.6g Protein; 11.2g Sugars

Ingredients

1/2 pound red beetroot, julienned
1/2 pound golden beetroot, julienned
1/4 pound carrot, julienned
Sea salt and ground black pepper, to taste
1 teaspoon olive oil
1/2 cup mayonnaise
1 teaspoon garlic, minced
1/4 teaspoon dried dill weed

Directions

Toss your veggies with salt, black pepper and olive oil.
Arrange the veggie chips in a single layer in the Air Fryer cooking basket.
Cook the veggie chips in the preheated Air Fryer at 340 degrees F for 20 minutes; tossing the basket occasionally to ensure even cooking. Work with two batches.
Meanwhile, mix the mayonnaise, garlic and dill until well combined.
Serve the vegetable chips with the mayo sauce on the side.

Greedy Wontons

(Ready in about 30 minutes | Servings 6)

445 Calories; 12.7g Fat; 50.8g Carbs; 32g Protein; 2.8g Sugars

Ingredients

1/2 pound ground turkey
1 teaspoon shallot powder
1 teaspoon instant dashi granules
1 teaspoon fish sauce
1 tablespoon tomato paste
1 teaspoon soy sauce
1 teaspoon sesame oil
Seas salt and ground black pepper, to taste 20 wonton wrappers, defrosted

Directions

Brush a nonstick skillet with cooking spray. Once hot, cook the ground turkey until no longer pink, crumbling with a fork. Stir in the other ingredients, except for the wonton wrappers; stir to combine well.
Place the wonton wrappers on a clean work surface. Divide the filling between wrappers. Wet the edge of each wrapper with water, fold top half over bottom half and pinch border to seal.
Cook your wontons at 400 degrees F for 8 minutes; working in batches.

Roasted Tofu

(Ready in about 30 minutes | Servings 6)

112 Calories; 6.6g Fat; 3.6g Carbs; 12.1g Protein; 0.2g Sugars

Ingredients

8 ounces firm tofu, pressed and cut into bite-sized cubes
1 tablespoon tamari sauce
1 teaspoon peanut oil
1/2 teaspoon garlic powder
1/2 teaspoon onion powder

Directions

Toss the tofu cubes with tamari sauce, peanut oil, garlic powder and onion powder.
Cook your tofu in the preheated Air Fryer at 380 degrees F for about 13 minutes, shaking the basket once or twice to ensure even browning.

Cake with walnuts

(Ready in about 50 minutes | Servings 6)

455 Calories; 25.4g Fat; 52.1g Carbs; 6.1g Protein; 15g Sugars

Ingredients

1 (10-ounces) can crescent rolls
1/2 stick butter
1/2 cup caster sugar
1 teaspoon pumpkin pie spice blend
1 tablespoon dark rum
1/2 cup walnuts, chopped

Directions

Start by preheating your Air Fryer to 350 degrees F.
Roll out the crescent rolls. Spread the butter onto the crescent rolls; scatter the sugar, spices and walnuts over the rolls. Drizzle with rum and roll them up.
Using your fingertips, gently press them to seal the edges.
Bake your cake for about 13 minutes or until the top is golden brown.

Chicken and Peppers

(Ready in about 45 minutes | Servings 3)

397 Calories; 18.8g Fat; 20.6g Carbs; 34.2g Protein; 3.1g Sugars

Ingredients

1/2 cup all-purpose four
1 teaspoon kosher salt
1 teaspoon shallot powder
1/2 teaspoon dried basil
1/2 teaspoon dried oregano
1/2 teaspoon smoked paprika
1 tablespoon hot sauce
1/4 cup mayonnaise
1/4 cup milk
1 pound chicken drumettes
1 bell peppers, sliced

Directions

In a shallow bowl, mix the flour, salt, shallot powder, basil, oregano and smoked paprika.

In another bowl, mix the hot sauce, mayonnaise and milk.

Dip the chicken drumettes in the flour mixture, then, coat them with the milk mixture; make sure to coat well on all sides.

Cook in the preheated Air Fryer at 380 degrees F for 28 to 30 minutes; turn them over halfway through the cooking time. Reserve chicken drumettes, keeping them warm.

Then, cook the peppers at 400 degrees F for 13 to 15 minutes, shaking the basket once or twice.

Pork with Brussels sprouts

(Ready in about 20 minutes | Servings 3)

381 Calories; 11.7g Fat; 14.1g Carbs; 56g Protein; 3.4g Sugars

Ingredients

1 pound Brussels sprouts, halved
1 ½ pounds tenderloin
1 teaspoon peanut oil
1 teaspoon garlic powder
1 tablespoon coriander, minced
1 teaspoon smoked paprika
Sea salt and ground black pepper, to taste

Directions

Toss the Brussels sprouts and pork with oil and spices until well coated.
Place in the Air Fryer cooking basket. Cook in the preheated Air Fryer at 370 degrees F for 15 minutes.
Taste and adjust seasonings. Eat warm.

Greek Style Roast Beef

(Ready in about 55 minutes | Servings 3)

348 Calories; 16.1g Fat; 1.6g Carbs; 49g Protein; 0.9g Sugars

Ingredients

1 clove garlic, halved
1 ½ pounds beef eye round roast
3 zucchini, sliced lengthwise
4 teaspoons olive oil
1 teaspoon Greek spice mix
Sea salt, to season
1/2 cup Greek-style yogurt

Directions

Rub the beef eye round roast with garlic halves.
Brush the beef eye round roast and zucchini with olive oil. Sprinkle with spices and place the beef in the cooking basket.
Roast in your Air Fryer at 400 degrees F for 40 minutes. Turn the beef over.
Add the zucchini to the cooking basket and continue to cook for 12 minutes more or until cooked through. Serve warm, garnished with Greek-style yogurt.

Squid with Southern Flavors

(Ready in about 10 minutes | Servings 2)

529 Calories; 24.3g Fat; 41g Carbs; 33.2g Protein; 3.2g Sugar

Ingredients

1/2 pound calamari tubes cut into rings, cleaned
Sea salt and ground black pepper, to season
1/2 cup almond flour
1/2 cup all-purpose flour
4 tablespoons parmesan cheese, grated
1/2 cup ale beer
1/4 teaspoon cayenne pepper
1/2 cup breadcrumbs
1/4 cup mayonnaise
1/4 cup Greek-style yogurt
1 clove garlic, minced
1 tablespoon fresh lemon juice
1 teaspoon fresh parsley, chopped
2 teaspoon fresh dill, chopped

Directions

Sprinkle the calamari with salt and black pepper.

Mix the flour, cheese and beer in a bowl until well combined. In another bowl, mix cayenne pepper and breadcrumbs

Dip the calamari pieces in the flour mixture, then roll them onto the breadcrumb mixture, pressing to coat on all sides; transfer them to a lightly oiled cooking basket.

Cook at 400 degrees F for 4 minutes, shaking the basket halfway through the cooking time.

Meanwhile, mix the remaining ingredients until everything is well incorporated. Serve warm calamari with the sauce for dipping.

Roasted Squash

(Ready in about 15 minutes | Servings 3)

189 Calories; 8.4g Fat; 22.3g Carbs; 6.7g Protein; 5.8g Sugars

Ingredients

1 pound acorn squash, peeled, seeded and cubed
1 teaspoon coconut oil, melted
1 tablespoon honey
1/4 teaspoon grated nutmeg
1/4 teaspoon ground cloves
1/2 teaspoon cinnamon powder
1/4 teaspoon ground white pepper
1/2 teaspoon dread dill weed
1/2 cup chèvre cheese, crumbled

Directions

Toss the acorn squash cubes with coconut oil, honey, nutmeg, cloves, cinnamon, white pepper and dill weed.
Transfer the acorn squash to a lightly greased cooking basket.
Cook the acorn squash in the preheated Air Fryer at 400 degrees F for 6 minutes; shake the basket and cook for a further 6 minutes.
Place the roasted squash on a serving platter, garnish with chèvre cheese and serve.

Pear in Chips with Cinnamon

(Ready in about 10 minutes | Servings 2)

94 Calories; 2.6g Fat; 18.1g Carbs; 0.7g Protein; 12.6g Sugars

Ingredients

1 large pear, cored and sliced
1 teaspoon apple pie spice blend
1 teaspoon coconut oil
1 teaspoon honey

Directions

Toss the pear slices with the spice blend, coconut oil and honey. Then, place the pear slices in the Air Fryer cooking basket and cook at 360 degrees F for about 8 minutes.

Shake the basket once or twice to ensure even cooking. Pear chips will crisp up as it cools.

Mac and Cheese

(Ready in about 25 minutes | Servings 2)

439 Calories; 24.4g Fat; 34.4g Carbs; 19.5g Protein; 3.6g Sugars

Ingredients

3/4 cup cavatappi
1/4 cup double cream
4 ounces Colby cheese, shredded
1/2 teaspoon granulated garlic
Sea salt and ground black pepper, to taste
1/4 teaspoon cayenne pepper

Directions

Bring a pot of salted water to a boil over high heat; turn the heat down to medium and add the cavatappi.
Let it simmer about 8 minutes. Drain cavatappi, reserving 1/4 cup of the cooking water; add them to a lightly greased baking pan.
Add in 1/4 cup of the cooking water, double cream, cheese and spices to the baking pan; gently stir to combine.
Bake your mac and cheese in the preheated Air Fryer at 360 degrees F for 15 minutes. Garnish with fresh basil leaves if desired.

Australian Style Pancakes

(Ready in about 30 minutes | Servings 4)

370 Calories; 5.8g Fat; 72.3g Carbs; 10.2g Protein; 48.2g Sugars

Ingredients

1/2 cup flour
A pinch of salt
A pinch of sugar
1/2 cup whole milk
3 eggs
1 shot of rum
4 tablespoons raisins
1/2 cup icing sugar
1/2 cup stewed plums

Directions

Mix the flour, salt, sugar, and milk in a bowl until the batter becomes semi-solid.
Fold in the eggs; add the rum and whisk to combine well. Let it stand for 20 minutes.
Spritz the Air Fryer baking pan with cooking spray. Pour the batter into the pan using a measuring cup. Scatter the raisins over the top. Cook at 230 degrees F for 4 to 5 minutes or until golden brown. Repeat with the remaining batter.
Cut the pancake into pieces, sprinkle over the icing sugar, and serve with the stewed plums.

Blueberry Pancakes with Raw Sugar

(Ready in about 20 minutes | Servings 4)

218 Calories; 6.6g Fat; 35.6g Carbs; 4.7g Protein; 22.5g Sugars

Ingredients

1/2 cup plain flour
1/2 teaspoon baking powder
1 teaspoon brown sugar
A pinch of grated nutmeg
1/4 teaspoon ground star anise
A pinch of salt
1 egg
1/4 cup coconut milk
1 cup fresh blueberries
1 tablespoon coconut oil, melted
4 tablespoons cinnamon sugar

Directions

Combine the flour, baking powder, brown sugar, nutmeg, star anise and salt. In another bowl, whisk the eggs and milk until frothy. Add the wet mixture to the dry mixture and mix to combine well. Fold in the fresh blueberries. Carefully place spoonfuls of batter into the Air Fryer cooking basket. Brush them with melted coconut oil.
Cook your fritters in the preheated Air Fryer at 370 degrees for 10 minutes, flipping them halfway through the cooking time. Repeat with the remaining batter.
Dust your fritters with the cinnamon sugar and serve at room temperature.

Turkey Breast with Garlic and Basil Scent

(Ready in about 45 minutes | Servings 4)

355 Calories; 18.7g Fat; 2.1g Carbs; 38g Protein; 0.7g Sugars

Ingredients

1 ½ pounds turkey breast
2 tablespoons olive oil
2 cloves garlic, minced
Sea salt and ground black pepper, to taste
1 teaspoon basil
2 tablespoons lemon zest, grated

Directions

Pat the turkey breast dry with paper towels.
Rub the turkey breast with olive oil, garlic, salt, pepper, basil and lemon zest.
Cook in the preheated Air Fryer at 380 degrees F for 20 minutes.
Turn the turkey breast over and cook an additional 20 to 22 minutes.

Pork Sausage and Potatoes

(Ready in about 35 minutes | Servings 3)

640 Calories; 47.5g Fat; 27.4g Carbs; 24.3g Protein; 1.1g Sugars

Ingredients

1 pound pork sausage, uncooked
1 pound baby potatoes
1/4 teaspoon paprika
1/2 teaspoon dried rosemary leaves, crushed
Himalayan salt and black pepper, to taste

Direction

Put the sausage into the Air Fryer cooking basket.
Cook in the preheated Air Fryer at 380 degrees F for 15 minutes; reserve.
Season the baby potatoes with paprika, rosemary, salt and black pepper. Add the baby potatoes to the cooking basket.
Cook the potatoes at 400 degrees F for 15 minutes, shaking the basket once or twice. Serve warm sausages with baby potatoes.

Masala Dum Kabab

(Ready in about 20 minutes | Servings 3)

313 Calories; 11.5g Fat; 2.8g Carbs; 49g Protein; 0.3g Sugars

Ingredients

1 ½ pounds ground beef
1/2 cup breadcrumbs
1 teaspoon garam masala
1 teaspoon garlic paste
1/2 teaspoon turmeric powder
1/2 teaspoon coriander powder
Sea salt and ground black pepper, to taste

Directions

In a mixing bowl, combine all ingredients. Divide the mixture into three pieces and roll them into kabab shape.
Spritz each kabab with a nonstick spray and place them in the cooking basket.
Cook in the preheated Air Fryer at 380 degrees F for 10 minutes.
Flip them over and cook an additional 5 minutes.
Serve immediately with warm chapati.

Peppers with Feta

(Ready in about 15 minutes | Servings 2)

249 Calories; 17.6g Fat; 12.3g Carbs; 12.1g Protein; 7.5g Sugars

Ingredients

4 bell peppers
1 teaspoon olive oil
1 teaspoon garlic, minced
1 tablespoon champagne vinegar
2 tablespoons fresh parsley, chopped
Kosher salt, to taste
5 ounces feta cheese, crumbled
2 tablespoons pine nuts, toasted

Directions

Brush the peppers with olive oil and place them in the Air Fryer cooking basket.
Roast the peppers at 400 degrees F for 15 minutes, turning your peppers over halfway through the cooking time; roast the peppers until the skin blisters and turns black.
Transfer the peppers to a plastic bag until cool.
Now, the skins should peel away off of the peppers easily. Slice the peppers into strips; stir in the garlic, vinegar, parsley and salt.
Toss to combine well and top with feta cheese and pine nuts.

Meatballs with Roman Cheese

(Ready in about 15 minutes | Servings 2)

264 Calories; 14.6g Fat; 3.7g Carbs; 29.7g Protein; 1.6g Sugars

Ingredients

1/2 pound ground turkey
2 tablespoons tomato ketchup
1 teaspoon stone-ground mustard
2 tablespoons scallions, chopped
1 garlic clove, minced
1/4 Pecorino-Romano cheese, grated
1 egg, beaten
1/2 teaspoon red pepper flakes, crushed
Sea salt and ground black pepper, to taste

Directions

In a mixing bowl, thoroughly combine all ingredients.
Shape the mixture into 6 equal meatballs. Transfer the meatballs to the Air Fryer cooking basket that is previously greased with a nonstick cooking spray.
Cook the meatballs at 360 degrees F for 10 to 11 minutes, shaking the basket occasionally to ensure even cooking. An instant thermometer should read 165 degrees F.

Turkey Burritos

(Ready in about 20 minutes | Servings 3)

580 Calories; 21.3g Fat; 65.6g Carbs; 31g Protein; 5.7g Sugars

Ingredients

1/2 pound ground turkey
1 teaspoon taco seasoning blend
1 teaspoon deli mustard
8 ounces canned black beans
1/2 red onion, sliced
Sea salt and ground black pepper, to taste
3 (12-inch) whole-wheat tortillas, warmed
1/2 cup Cotija cheese, crumbled
1 cup butterhead lettuce, torn into pieces
1 teaspoon olive oil

Directions

Cook the ground turkey in a nonstick skillet for about 4 minutes, crumbling with a fork. Stir the taco seasoning blend, mustard, beans, onion, salt and pepper into the skillet.

Place the meat mixture in the center of each tortilla. Top with cheese and lettuce. Roll your tortillas to make burritos.

Brush each burrito with olive oil and place them in the lightly greased cooking basket. Bake your burritos at 395 degrees F for 10 minutes, turning them over halfway through the cooking time.

Serve immediately with salsa on the side, if desired.

Tofu with Brussels sprouts

(Ready in about 20 minutes | Servings 2)

256 Calories; 12.5g Fat; 21.1g Carbs; 22.8g Protein; 3.6g Sugars

Ingredients

8 ounces firm tofu, pressed and cut into bite-sized cubes
1 teaspoon garlic paste
1 tablespoons arrowroot powder
1 teaspoon peanut oil
1/2 pound Brussels sprouts, halved
Sea salt and ground black pepper, to taste

Directions

Toss the tofu cubes with the garlic paste, arrowroot powder and peanut oil.

Transfer your tofu to the Air Fryer cooking basket; add in the Brussels sprouts and season everything with salt and black pepper.

Cook the tofu cubes and Brussels sprouts at 380 degrees F for 15 minutes, shaking the basket halfway through the cooking time.

Blueberry Pancakes

(Ready in about 20 minutes | Servings 4)

218 Calories; 6.6g Fat; 35.6g Carbs; 4.7g Protein; 22.5g Sugars

Ingredients

1/2 cup plain flour
1/2 teaspoon baking powder
1 teaspoon brown sugar
A pinch of grated nutmeg
1/4 teaspoon ground star anise
A pinch of salt
1 egg
1/4 cup coconut milk
1 cup fresh blueberries
1 tablespoon coconut oil, melted
4 tablespoons cinnamon sugar

Directions

Combine the flour, baking powder, brown sugar, nutmeg, star anise and salt. In another bowl, whisk the eggs and milk until frothy. Add the wet mixture to the dry mixture and mix to combine well. Fold in the fresh blueberries. Carefully place spoonfuls of batter into the Air Fryer cooking basket. Brush them with melted coconut oil.

Cook your fritters in the preheated Air Fryer at 370 degrees for 10 minutes, flipping them halfway through the cooking time. Repeat with the remaining batter. Dust your fritters with the cinnamon sugar and serve at room temperature.

Molten Chocolate Cake

(Ready in about 12 minutes | Servings 2)

405 Calories; 29.5g Fat; 30.1g Carbs; 5.1g Protein; 23.1g Sugars

Ingredients

1/2 cup dark chocolate chunks
3 tablespoons butter
1 egg
1 ounce granulated sugar
1 tablespoon self-rising flour
2 tablespoons almonds, chopped

Directions

Microwave the chocolate chunks and butter for 30 to 40 seconds until the mixture is smooth.
Then, beat the eggs and sugar; stir in the egg mixture into the chocolate mixture. Now, stir in the flour and almonds.
Pour the batter into two ramekins.
Bake your cakes at 370 degrees for about 10 minutes and serve at room temperature.

Thanksgiving Day

(Ready in about 55 minutes | Servings 4)

356 Calories; 18g Fat; 7.8g Carbs; 34.2g Protein; 0.6g Sugars

Ingredients

1 ½ pound turkey breast
1 tablespoon Dijon mustard
2 tablespoons butter, at room temperature
Sea salt and ground black pepper, to taste
1 teaspoon cayenne pepper
1/2 teaspoon garlic powder
Gravy:
2 cups vegetable broth
1/4 cup all-purpose flour
Freshly ground black pepper, to taste

Directions

Brush Dijon mustard and butter all over the turkey breast. Season with salt, black pepper, cayenne pepper and garlic powder.
Cook in the preheated Air Fryer at 360 degrees F for about 50 minutes, flipping them halfway through the cooking time.
Place the fat drippings from the cooked turkey in a sauté pan. Pour in 1 cup of broth and 1/8 cup of all-purpose flour; continue to cook, whisking continuously, until a smooth paste forms.
Add in the remaining ingredients and continue to simmer until the gravy has reduced by half.

Goulash

(Ready in about 45 minutes | Servings 2)

474 Calories; 27.1g Fat; 10g Carbs; 44.5g Protein; 5.7g Sugars

Ingredients

1/2 pound pork stew meat, cut into bite-sized chunks
2 pork good quality sausages, sliced
1 small onion, sliced into rings
2 Italian peppers, sliced
1 Serrano pepper, sliced
2 garlic cloves, minced
1 tablespoon soy sauce
1/2 teaspoon ground cumin
1 bay leaf
Salt and black pepper, to taste
1 cup beef stock

Directions

Place the pork and sausage in the Air Fryer cooking basket. Cook the meat at 380 degrees F for 15 minutes, shaking the basket once or twice; place in a heavy-bottomed pot.

Now, add the onion and peppers to the cooking basket; cook your vegetables at 400 degrees F for 10 minutes and transfer to the pot with the pork and sausage.

Add in the remaining ingredients and cook, partially covered, for 15 to 20 minutes until everything is cooked through.

Spoon into individual bowls and serve.

Meat Burritos

(Ready in about 25 minutes | Servings 3)

368 Calories; 13g Fat; 20.2g Carbs; 35.1g Protein; 2.7g Sugars

Ingredients

1 pound rump steak
Sea salt and crushed red pepper, to taste
1/2 teaspoon shallot powder
1/2 teaspoon porcini powder
1/2 teaspoon celery seeds
1/2 teaspoon dried Mexican oregano
1 teaspoon piri piri powder
1 teaspoon lard, melted
3 (approx 7-8" dia) whole-wheat tortillas

Directions

Toss the rump steak with the spices and melted lard.
Cook in your Air Fryer at 390 degrees F for 20 minutes, turning it halfway through the cooking time. Place on a cutting board to cool slightly.
Slice against the grain into thin strips.
Spoon the beef strips onto wheat tortillas; top with your favorite fixings, roll them up and serve.

Fish Sticks

(Ready in about 12 minutes | Servings 2)

571 Calories; 41.7g Fat; 36.2g Carbs; 14.2g Protein; 9.2g Sugars

Ingredients

1/2 pound fish sticks, frozen
1/2 pound Vidalia onions, halved
1 teaspoon sesame oil
Sea salt and ground black pepper, to taste
1/2 teaspoon red pepper flakes
4 tablespoons mayonnaise
4 tablespoons Greek-style yogurt
1/4 teaspoon mustard seeds
1 teaspoon chipotle chili in adobo, minced

Directions

Drizzle the fish sticks and Vidalia onions with sesame oil. Toss them with salt, black pepper and red pepper flakes.
Transfer them to the Air Fryer cooking basket.
Cook the fish sticks and onions at 400 degreed F for 5 minutes.
Shake the basket and cook an additional 5 minutes or until cooked through.
Meanwhile, mix the mayonnaise, Greek-style yogurt, mustard seeds and chipotle chili.
Serve the warm fish sticks garnished with Vidalia onions and the sauce on the side.

Brussels Sprouts and Feta Together

(Ready in about 15 minutes | Servings 3)

177 Calories; 7.3g Fat; 22.3g Carbs; 9.1g Protein; 10.1g Sugars

Ingredients

1 pound Brussels sprouts
1 teaspoon olive oil
Sea salt and ground black pepper, to taste
1/4 teaspoon red pepper flakes
1 tablespoon balsamic vinegar
1 tablespoon molasses
1/2 teaspoon dried dill weed
1/2 teaspoon granulated garlic
1/2 cup feta cheese, crumbled

Directions

Toss the Brussels sprouts with olive oil, salt, black pepper, red pepper, balsamic vinegar, molasses, dill and garlic.
Cook the Brussels sprouts in the preheated Air Fryer at 380 degrees F for 15 minutes, shaking the basket halfway through the cooking time to ensure even browning.
Place in a serving platter and serve with feta cheese.

Tomato Chips

(Ready in about 20 minutes | Servings 2)

119 Calories; 6.5g Fat; 9.1g Carbs; 6.6g Protein; 1.4g Sugars

Ingredients

1 tomatoes, cut into thick rounds
1 teaspoon extra-virgin olive oil
Sea salt and fresh ground pepper, to taste
1 teaspoon Italian seasoning mix
1/4 cup Romano cheese, grated

Directions

Start by preheating your Air Fryer to 350 degrees F.
Toss the tomato sounds with remaining ingredients. Transfer the tomato rounds to the cooking basket without overlapping.
Cook your tomato rounds in the preheated Air Fryer for 5 minutes. Flip them over and cook an additional 5 minutes. Work with batches.

Mac and Cheese

(Ready in about 25 minutes | Servings 2)

439 Calories; 24.4g Fat; 34.4g Carbs; 19.5g Protein; 3.6g Sugars

Ingredients

3/4 cup cavatappi
1/4 cup double cream
4 ounces Colby cheese, shredded
1/2 teaspoon granulated garlic
Sea salt and ground black pepper, to taste
1/4 teaspoon cayenne pepper

Directions

Bring a pot of salted water to a boil over high heat; turn the heat down to medium and add the cavatappi.

Let it simmer about 8 minutes. Drain cavatappi, reserving 1/4 cup of the cooking water; add them to a lightly greased baking pan.

Add in 1/4 cup of the cooking water, double cream, cheese and spices to the baking pan; gently stir to combine.

Bake your mac and cheese in the preheated Air Fryer at 360 degrees F for 15 minutes. Garnish with fresh basil leaves if desired.

Golden Eggplant

(Ready in about 45 minutes | Servings 3)

214 Calories; 1.3g Fat; 43g Carbs; 6.1g Protein; 16.8g Sugars

Ingredients

1 pound eggplant, cut lengthwise into 1/2-inch thick slices
1/4 cup plain flour
1/4 cup almond milk
1 cup fresh bread crumbs
1 teaspoon Cajun seasoning mix
Sea salt and ground black pepper, to taste
1 cup tomato sauce
1 teaspoon brown mustard
1/2 teaspoon chili powder

Directions

Toss your eggplant with 1 teaspoon of salt and leave it for 30 minutes; drain and rinse the eggplant and set it aside.
In a shallow bowl, mix the flour with almond milk until well combined. In a separate bowl, mix the breadcrumbs with Cajun seasoning mix, salt and black pepper.
Dip your eggplant in the flour mixture, then, coat each slice with the breadcrumb mixture, pressing to adhere.
Cook the breaded eggplant at 400 degrees F for 10 minutes, flipping them halfway through the cooking time to ensure even browning.
In the meantime, mix the remaining ingredients for the sauce. Divide the tomato mixture between eggplant cutlets and continue to cook for another 5 minutes or until thoroughly cooked.
Transfer the warm eggplant cutlets to a wire rack to stay crispy.

Classic Chocolate Cake

(Ready in about 10 minutes | Servings 2)

546 Calories; 34.1g Fat; 55.4g Carbs; 11.4g Protein; 25.7g Sugars

Ingredients

1/2 cup self-rising flour
6 tablespoons brown sugar
5 tablespoons coconut milk
4 tablespoons coconut oil
4 tablespoons unsweetened cocoa powder
2 eggs
A pinch of grated nutmeg
A pinch of salt

Directions

Mix all the ingredients together; divide the batter between two mugs. Place the mugs in the Air Fryer cooking basket and cook at 390 degrees F for about 10 minutes.

Greek Meatballs

(Ready in about 15 minutes | Servings 2)

493 Calories; 27.9g Fat; 27.1g Carbs; 32.6g Protein; 4.2g Sugars

Ingredients

1/2 pound ground chicken
1 egg
1 slice stale bread, cubed and soaked in milk
1 teaspoon fresh garlic, pressed
2 tablespoons Romano cheese, grated
1 bell pepper, deveined and chopped
1 teaspoon olive oil
1/2 teaspoon dried oregano
1/2 teaspoon dried basil
1/8 teaspoon grated nutmeg
Sea salt and ground black pepper, to taste
2 pita bread

Directions

Thoroughly combine all ingredients, except for the pita bread, in a mixing bowl. Stir until everything is well incorporated.
Roll the mixture into 6 meatballs and place them in a lightly oiled cooking basket.
Air fry at 380 degrees F for 10 minutes, shaking the basket occasionally to ensure even cooking.
Place the keftedes in a pita bread and serve with tomato and tzatziki sauce if desired.

Pork with Roasted Peppers

(Ready in about 55 minutes | Servings 3)

409 Calories; 20.1g Fat; 4.3g Carbs; 49g Protein; 2.4g Sugars

Ingredients

1 red bell peppers
1 ½ pounds pork loin
1 garlic clove, halved
1 teaspoon lard, melted
1/2 teaspoon cayenne pepper
1/4 teaspoon cumin powder
1/4 teaspoon ground bay laurel
Kosher salt and ground black pepper, to taste

Directions

Roast the peppers in the preheated Air Fryer at 395 degrees F for 10 minutes, flipping them halfway through the cooking time.
Let them steam for 10 minutes; then, peel the skin and discard the stems and seeds. Slice the peppers into halves and add salt to taste.
Rub the pork with garlic; brush with melted lard and season with spices until well coated on all sides.
Place in the cooking basket and cook at 360 digress F for 25 minutes. Turn the meat over and cook an additional 20 minutes.
Serve with roasted peppers.

American Roast Beef

(Ready in about 30 minutes | Servings 3)

294 Calories; 10.9g Fat; 0.3g Carbs; 45.9g Protein; 0.3g Sugars

Ingredients

1 pound beef eye of round roast
1 teaspoon sesame oil
1 teaspoon red pepper flakes
1/4 teaspoon dried bay laurel
1/2 teaspoon cumin powder
Sea salt and black pepper, to taste
1 sprig thyme, crushed

Directions

Simply toss the beef with the remaining ingredients; toss until well coated on all sides.
Cook in the preheated Air Fryer at 390 degrees F for 15 to 20 minutes, flipping the meat halfway through to cook on the other side.
Remove from the cooking basket, cover loosely with foil and let rest for 15 minutes before carving and serving.

Meatballs with Fish and Peppers

(Ready in about 15 minutes | Servings 3)

226 Calories; 6.5g Fat; 10.9g Carbs; 31.4g Protein; 2.6g Sugars

Ingredients

1 pound haddock
1 egg
2 tablespoons milk
1 bell pepper, deveined and finely chopped
2 stalks fresh scallions, minced
1/2 teaspoon fresh garlic, minced
Sea salt and ground black pepper, to taste
1/2 teaspoon cumin seeds
1/4 teaspoon celery seeds
1/2 cup breadcrumbs
1 teaspoon olive oil

Directions

Thoroughly combine all ingredients, except for the breadcrumbs and olive oil, until everything is blended well.

Then, roll the mixture into 3 patties and coat them with breadcrumbs, pressing to adhere. Drizzle olive oil over the patties and transfer them to the Air Fryer cooking basket.

Cook the fish cakes at 400 degrees F for 5 minutes; turn them over and continue to cook an additional 5 minutes until cooked through.

Zucchini Pancakes

(Ready in about 20 minutes | Servings 3)

227 Calories; 11.5g Fat; 19.2g Carbs; 10.3g Protein; 1.9g Sugars

Ingredients

2 medium zucchini, shredded and drained
1 teaspoon Italian seasoning mix
Sea salt and ground black pepper, to taste
1/2 yellow onion, finely chopped
1 teaspoon garlic, finely chopped
1/2 cup plain flour
1 large egg, beaten
1/2 cup Asiago cheese, shredded
1 teaspoon olive oil

Directions

In a mixing bowl, thoroughly combine the zucchini, spices, yellow onion, garlic, flour, egg and Asiago cheese.

Shape the mixture into patties and brush them with olive oil; transfer the patties to a lightly oiled cooking basket.

Cook the patties in the preheated Air Fryer at 380 degrees F for 15 minutes, turning them over once or twice to ensure even cooking.

Garnish with some extra cheese if desired and serve at room temperature.

Pear Chips

(Ready in about 10 minutes | Servings 2)

94 Calories; 2.6g Fat; 18.1g Carbs; 0.7g Protein; 12.6g Sugars

Ingredients

1 large pear, cored and sliced
1 teaspoon apple pie spice blend
1 teaspoon coconut oil
3 teaspoon honey

Directions

Toss the pear slices with the spice blend, coconut oil and honey. Then, place the pear slices in the Air Fryer cooking basket and cook at 360 degrees F for about 8 minutes.

Shake the basket once or twice to ensure even cooking. Pear chips will crisp up as it cools.

Monkey Bread

(Ready in about 15 minutes | Servings 3)

270 Calories; 9.5g Fat; 33.6g Carbs; 11.2g Protein; 6.1g Sugars

Ingredients

6 ounces refrigerated crescent rolls
¼ cup ketchup
¼ cup pesto sauce
½ cup provolone cheese, shredded
2 cloves garlic, minced
½ teaspoon dried oregano
½ teaspoon dried basil
½ teaspoon dried parsley flakes

Directions

Start by preheating your Air Fryer to 350 degrees F.
Roll out crescent rolls. Divide the ingredients between crescent rolls and roll them up. Using your fingertips, gently press them to seal the edges.
Bake the mini monkey bread for 12 minutes or until the top is golden brown.

Beet with Tahini Sauce

(Ready in about 40 minutes | Servings 2)

253 Calories; 18.1g Fat; 19.1g Carbs; 6.4g Protein; 10.1g Sugars

Ingredients

2 golden beets
1 tablespoon sesame oil
Sea salt and ground black pepper, to taste
2 cups baby spinach
2 tablespoons tahini
2 tablespoons soy sauce
1 tablespoon white vinegar
1 clove garlic, pressed
1/2 jalapeno pepper, chopped
1/4 teaspoon ground cumin

Directions

Toss the golden beets with sesame oil. Cook the golden beets in the preheated Air Fryer at 400 degrees F for 40 minutes, turning them over once or twice to ensure even cooking.
Let your beets cool completely and then, slice them with a sharp knife. Place the beets in a salad bowl and add in salt, pepper and baby spinach.
In a small mixing dish, whisk the remaining ingredients until well combined.
Spoon the sauce over your beets, toss to combine and serve immediately.

253 Calories; 18.1g Fat; 19.1g Carbs; 6.4g Protein; 10.1g Sugars

Fried Cupcakes

(Ready in about 10 minutes | Servings 4)

255 Calories; 7.6g Fat; 42.1g Carbs; 5g Protein; 17.1g Sugars

Ingredients

8 ounces bread dough
2 tablespoons butter, melted
4 ounces powdered sugar

Directions

Cut the dough into strips and twist them together 3 to 4 times. Then, brush the dough twists with melted butter and sprinkle sugar over them.

Cook the dough twists at 350 degrees F for 8 minutes, tossing the basket halfway through the cooking time.

Serve with your favorite dip.

CPSIA information can be obtained
at www.ICGtesting.com
Printed in the USA
LVHW051748250621
691051LV00009B/809

9 781802 751567